WHAT CHRIST THINKS OF THE CHURCH

What Christ Thinks of the Church

Insights from Revelation 2-3

JOHN R. W. STOTT

WILLIAM B. EERDMANS PUBLISHING COMPANY
GRAND RAPIDS, MICHIGAN

First American Edition, April 1958
Sixth Printing, February 1980

Library of Congress Catalog Card number: 58-9548

ISBN 0-8028-1451-4

PHOTOLITHOPRINTED BY EERDMANS PRINTING COMPANY
GRAND RAPIDS, MICHIGAN, UNITED STATES OF AMERICA

CONTENTS

N

TROAS

PERGAMUM

THYATIRA

SARDIS

SMYRNA

PHILADELPHIA

EPHESUS

LAODICEA

COLOSSAE

MILETUS

PATMOS

ASIA   MINOR

– – – – ROMAN ROAD

SCALE 0   60 MLS

THE SEVEN CHURCHES OF ASIA

FOREWORD

WHAT Christ thinks of the Church is a question which no professing Christian can afford to ignore. What Christians think of it from inside and what unbelievers think of it from outside are both important subjects for consideration; but far more significant is the opinion of Jesus Christ Himself, the Church's Founder and Lord.

We must be deeply thankful that, in seeking to discover Christ's view of the Church, we do not have to work in the dark. The New Testament supplies us with much information concerning our Lord's purposes for His Church. We may glean from some of His own words as recorded in the Gospels, from the description of the primitive Church given us in the Acts, and from the epistles to various churches in the rest of the New Testament just what is His plan for the Church which is His body.

No passage in the New Testament, however, contains more clear, concise and comprehensive instruction on the Church's life and work than the second and third chapters of the Book of Revelation. Here are written messages to seven of the most prominent churches of the Roman Province of Asia. Though penned by the hand of St. John, it is claimed that these letters emanate directly from the lips of the ascended and glorified Jesus Christ. In them, by praise and censure, warning and exhortation, He makes plain much of His will for His people, the more so when the letters are read not in isolation but in the context of the first seven chapters of the Revelation in which they are embedded.

It is my humble and earnest prayer that the chapters which follow, first given in embryo as a series of sermons in All Souls

Church, Langham Place, during Lent 1957, and now elaborated, will stir some Christians to examine the life of the Church today in the light of the pure ideal of the Church's Head. We shall find much in Christ's letters to the first century Asian churches to call us to repentance and renewal; much to humble and shame us; much to warn us of the wiles of the enemy; and much to incite us to fortitude and perseverance. May our ears be opened to hear "what the Spirit says to the churches".

The text used is taken from the (American) Revised Standard Version, and sentences printed in italics are quotations from the passage under consideration.

J. R. W. S.

"The Revelation of Jesus Christ"
Rev. 1: 1
"I saw . . . in the midst of the lampstands
one like a son of man" Rev. 1: 12, 13

I

INTRODUCTION

THE average Christian fights shy of the Book of Revelation. It seems to him wellnigh incomprehensible. He is perhaps sceptical of some fanciful interpretations he has heard, and he cannot easily accustom himself to the book's bizarre imagery. To start reading the Revelation is to step into a strange, unfamiliar world of angels and demons, of lambs, lions, horses and dragons. Seals are broken, trumpets blown and the contents of seven bowls poured out on the earth. Two particularly malicious beasts appear, one emerging out of the sea with ten horns and seven heads, and the other rising from the earth with a lamb's horns and a dragon's voice. There is thunder, lightning, hail, fire, blood and smoke. The whole book appears at first sight to contain a chaotic profusion of weird and mysterious visions.

But we cannot leave the matter there. The book claims to be a divine revelation, given by God to His servants (1: 1). It promises at its beginning a special blessing to him who reads it aloud in church and to those who listen (1: 3), and it adds at the end a solemn warning to anyone who dares to tamper with its message, either by addition or by subtraction (22: 18–19). Besides, this last book of the Bible has been cherished by Christ's Church in every generation and has brought its challenge and its comfort to thousands of Christian believers. We should therefore be foolish to neglect it.

We are concerned here with the book's first three chapters, and in particular with the second and third chapters which contain seven letters addressed by the ascended Christ to seven Asian churches. Chapter one is introductory to the whole book, and to it we now turn. Indeed, some important clues to a right interpretation of the book are given us in its very first verse: *The revelation of Jesus Christ, which God gave Him to show to His servants what must soon take place; and He made it known by sending His angel to His servant John.* The first word in the Greek sentence is *apocalupsis*, which (like its Latin equivalent, *revelatio*) means an "unveiling". The whole book is a revelation, an unveiling by God's hand of truths which otherwise would have remained hidden.

(1) IT IS A REVELATION TO THE CHURCH

It will be helpful to begin with the simple observation that the revelation was made to the Church. The "apocalypse" or "revelation" was given by God *to His servants*. They were its recipients. It was granted for their benefit. This being so, it is absurd to give up trying to understand it. We must persevere.

Ostensibly the revelation which John was given and instructed to write in a book was intended for *the seven churches that are in Asia* (v. 4). A little later he names them. He is to send the book *to Ephesus and to Smyrna and to Pergamum and to Thyatira and to Sardis and to Philadelphia and to Laodicea* (v. 11). By "Asia" then is not meant the whole continent, nor even what we sometimes call "Asia Minor", but the Roman province of Asia which was located on the western seaboard of what we now know as Turkey. The seven cities mentioned form an irregular circle, and are listed in the order in which a messenger might visit them if commissioned to deliver the letters. Sailing from the island of Patmos, to which John had been banished, he would arrive at Ephesus. He would then travel north to Smyrna and Pergamum, south-east to Thyatira, Sardis and Philadelphia, and finish his journey at Laodicea. He would need only to keep to what Professor William Ramsay called "the great circular road that bound together the most populous, wealthy and influential part of the Province, the west-central region" (*The Letters to the Seven Churches of Asia*, p. 183).

This historical context for the Book of Revelation, however, cannot possibly be thought to exhaust its significance. Just as the letters of Paul to the Corinthians and the Thessalonians convey the word of God to us as well as to them, to London and New York and Cairo as well as to Corinth and Thessalonica, so Christ's letters through John to the first century Christian communities of Asia have a permanent value and a universal message. Commentators have not failed to notice that the Asian churches numbered seven, a number indicating perfection and completeness in a book whose numerals are nearly always symbolical. The seven churches of Asia, though historical, represent the local churches of all ages and of all lands.

The Christian society in the Roman province of Asia at that time was hard pressed. It is probable that the Revelation reflects the situation during the reign of the Emperor Domitian, who carried to its second stage the persecution of Christians begun twenty-five years previously by Nero. Nero's persecutions had been sporadic; Domitian's seem to have been more systematic. The effects of Nero's antagonism were felt in Rome only, while under Domitian, who was hungry for divine honours, the persecution spread to Asia. Christians who worshipped the Lord Christ were being invited to worship the Lord Caesar. The battle was joined. The hearts of Christians were filled with alarm. Already some of their number were receiving personal insults. Others were being boycotted in business. One or two had even lost their lives. Could the Church survive the storm which seemed to be on the point of breaking?

Persecution was not the only peril to which the churches of Asia were exposed. There was also error to be refuted and evil to be overcome. False prophets were abroad, who were contriving to deceive even established Christians by their heretical philosophies. Immoral men and women too were contaminating the Church by their influence, and standards of behaviour were being lowered.

Persecution, error and sin. These were not just inexplicable phenomena. St. John recognized their source with a clarity of insight which we badly need to recapture today. The devil was at work. Behind the outward situation in the Asian churches an invisible conflict raged between Christ and Antichrist, between the Lamb and the Dragon, between "the holy city" Jerusalem (the Church) and "the great city" Babylon (the world). The devil's assault upon Christ's Church was a pincer movement. He attacked from several directions. Now the onslaught was physical, through a persecuting emperor and his deputies. Now it was intellectual, through false cults, and now moral through sub-Christian ethical standards. These were the devil's three strategies, symbolically represented in the Revelation as the dragon's three allies: the beast from the sea, the beast from the earth (or the false prophet) and the harlot Babylon.

In every age it has been the same. The devil's tactics do not change. As we look round the world today, the same pressures are harassing different churches. In some areas of the world open hostility to the gospel is accompanied by physical violence. In others the Church is wrestling in intellectual combat with an insidious ideology or a materialistic philosophy with which it cannot come to terms. Elsewhere the struggle is in the moral field, as the world seeks to cajole the Church into conformity to its own ways.

The Book of Revelation begins to be intelligible only when it is seen as God's word to His servants in this situation. It is a message to the Church in the world. It is a call to us to endure tribulation, to hold fast to the truth, to resist the blandishments of the devil and to obey the commandments of God.

(2) IT IS A REVELATION OF JESUS CHRIST

If the recipients of the revelation are the churches of Christ, the substance of the revelation is Christ Himself. The book begins by describing itself as *a revelation of Jesus Christ*, and ends in its last two verses with echoes of His name (22: 20, 21). To call it "the Revelation of St. John the Divine" is thoroughly misleading. The revelation is indeed given *to* John; but it is *of* Christ. He is Himself its grand theme.

Now it is exactly this that the Church needs. A church with its back to the wall, fighting for survival, needs more than moral exhortation and pious entreaty; it must see Christ. A history of the world in cipher (which some Christians believe the Revelation to be) is cold comfort in comparison with a vision of the exalted Christ. The whole book concerns Him. Nobody can read it without gaining a clearer view of Him.

The first chapter makes this fact particularly plain. When He is first introduced, He is given an impressive list of three titles, to which is added a statement both of His past achievement and of His future triumph (vv. 5–7). He is *the faithful witness*. Is the Church called to bear witness in the world? Let it follow the example of its Lord. He said He had come into the world to bear witness to the truth (Jn.18: 37) and all through His ministry He was faithful. He spoke of what He knew and bore witness to what He had seen, and "in His testimony before Pontius Pilate made the good confession" (Jn. 3: 11; 1 Tim. 6: 13). He never faltered, even when He suffered. We must be faithful in our witness too.

Next, He is called *the first-born of the dead*. Others had been brought back to this life, but He was the first to enter a new and indestructible life. Others had returned to life, only to die again. He rose and is *alive for evermore*. He is now *the living one* (v. 18); death has no further dominion over Him. A persecuted church facing the possibility of martyrdom urgently needs this assurance.

He is also named *the ruler of kings on earth*. Earthly kings might seek to crush the Church, but Jesus Christ is King of kings. Human lords might try to domineer the lives of Christians, but Christ is Lord of lords. He directs the affairs and destinies of men and nations. He rules the kings on earth. His empire is wider than the sway of Rome. His dominion is universal.

To these three titles John adds in an eloquent doxology a description of our Lord's achievements, past and future. Not only does He love us; not only has He *freed us from our sins by His blood*; but He has *made us a kingdom*. Just as God entered into a covenant with the Israelites at Mount Sinai and made them His people, His kingdom over whom He ruled, so Christ by His death has ratified a new covenant and inaugurated a new Kingdom. The Christian Church is the new theocracy. Christ reigns over us. We are His Kingdom. Moreover, as in the old Israel so in the new, the members of God's Kingdom are "priests", enjoying intimate access to Him and offering Him the spiritual sacrifice of our worship.

He who has redeemed us and made us a Kingdom is one day *coming with the clouds, and every eye will see Him, every one who pierced Him; and all tribes of the earth will wail on account of Him* (v. 7). The eyes that now view Him with contempt will see Him then with terror. He is coming in judgment. He will put wrongs to right and redress the uneven balance of this present world. Let Christians lift up their heads! The day of their redemption is drawing near.

Such is the opening revelation of Jesus Christ in His titles and His deeds. It is but a foretaste of the richer disclosures which follow.

John goes on to write how on a certain Sunday during his exile he was granted an ecstatic vision of Jesus. He describes the details of what He saw, and each part is meaningful. At the same time, it is important to remember that the imagery he uses is intended to be symbolical rather than pictorial. The various elements in the vision are significant symbols to be interpreted, rather than actual features to be imagined. For example, if John saw Jesus with a sharp two-edged sword issuing from His mouth, we are not so much to visualize this literally as to remember that the words which Christ speaks are as sharp and piercing as a sword.

John's attention was drawn to the presence of Jesus by a loud voice behind him. Turning round, he *saw seven golden lampstands* and in the middle of them *one like a son of man* (vv. 12, 13). That is to say, he saw a human figure, and yet the person he saw was more than a mere man. He was glorious and sublime. He was like the son of man in Daniel's vision. He was in fact the glorified "man Christ Jesus". John at once noticed His clothes, for He was invested with the long robe and golden girdle of a priest or king or judge. His appearance was not only distinguished but venerable and holy for His hair was as white as wool or snow. His scrutiny was intense as His eyes flashed with the fire of judgment, and His feet were as strong as burnished brass. His voice thundered like the breakers which dashed themselves against the rocky coast of Patmos, and His face was as radiant as the sun (vv. 13-15).

The purpose of this vision was not the private enlightenment of John. The seer was to be allowed no personal monopoly of its riches. The vision was for the whole Church. John was given it in order to transmit it to others. *Write what you see in a book*, he was told, *and send it to the seven churches* (v. 11). So at the beginning of each of the seven letters Christ announces Himself as its original author and describes Himself by one or more of the features already revealed either in the titles or in the vision of this first chapter.

This visionary manifestation of Christ was too much for John to endure. It had been deafening to his ears and dazzling to his eyes. He *fell at His feet as though dead* (v. 17). But Jesus laid His hand on John's shoulder and said to him reassuringly "Fear not".

Rising to his feet, John could now absorb the immediate

message which Christ had to convey. The Lord affirmed His victory over death, commanded John to write in a book what he had seen and would yet see (vv. 18, 19), and then interpreted the two most prominent features of the vision, which I have not yet mentioned. These concern the seven lampstands among which Jesus stood, and the seven stars which He held in His right hand. Indeed, when John first turned round and saw the vision, it was on the lampstands rather than on Christ that his eye fell (v. 12). He did not see a candelabrum consisting of one lampstand with seven branches (such as stood in the tabernacle outside the veil). He saw seven separate lampstands, each no doubt with a lighted lamp, and Jesus Christ among them in the midst. *The seven lampstands*, Jesus explained, stood for *the seven churches*, and *the seven stars* for *the angels of the seven churches* (v. 20).

What these "angels" were, we cannot say for certain. They may have been the heavenly representatives and guardians of the churches, or they were perhaps the presiding ministers or "bishops" of the churches. What is clear is that both stars and lamps diffuse light, even if in different degree. So Christ's churches are meant to be light-bearers in the darkness of the world. No one can disperse the shadows of sin and sorrow but He who is the Light of the World and they to whom He graciously gave His own title. "You are the light of the world", He said in the sermon on the mount, ". . . let your light . . . shine . . ." (Jn. 8: 12; Mt. 5: 14, 16). But the Church's light is as borrowed as the moon's. If the stars are to shine and the lamps are to burn, they must remain in Christ's hand and in Christ's presence.

(3) IT IS A REVELATION THROUGH JOHN

Our account of the first chapter of the Apocalypse would not be complete if we gave the impression that Christ's message to the Church was immediate and direct. It was not. It was given through John. It was indeed a revelation of Christ to His Church, but John was the means of its transmission. *He made it known . . . to His servant John* (v. 1). Christ's command to write the visions in a book and send it to the seven churches is repeated twice (vv. 11 and 19), and occurs again at the threshold of each separate epistle. Each letter begins with the formula: "To the angel of the church in —— write . . ."

There is much debate and some dispute among scholars as to the identity of the human author of the Revelation. In this book I am assuming the traditional view that the writer who describes himself as plain "John", without any further clarification, is the apostle, the beloved disciple, the son of Zebedee and brother of James, who survived the other apostles and lived to a ripe old age as leader of the church of Ephesus. Certainly the author of this book possesses an authority which the churches of Asia recognized and an intimate knowledge of their geographical, social and spiritual condition.

His relationship with them is made closer by his sufferings. *I John, your brother*, he writes, *share with you in Jesus the tribulation and the kingdom and the patient endurance* (v. 9). He is on the island of Patmos, neither as a visitor nor as a missionary, but as an exile. To this "barren, rocky island about ten miles long and five wide" (R. H. Charles) he has been banished *on account of the word of God and the testimony of Jesus*. He has been bold in preaching God's word and faithful in his testimony to Jesus, and he has had to suffer for it. He has not escaped the tribulation which is engulfing the churches of Asia. But if he shares the suffering, he shares the glory too. He knows himself to be already a member of Christ's kingdom, just as they are, and he is learning the same constancy and fortitude in his trial which he earnestly desires for them.

It is to such a man, called, chosen and faithful, a partaker of Christ's sufferings and kingdom and patience, that this wonderful revelation is given. It is a revelation of Christ. It is addressed to the churches. The book is a revelation of Christ through John to the Church.

What Christ thinks of His Church and what He says to His Church we shall discover in detail in the next chapters. He has a right to think and say what He does. In the first place, it is His Church. He founded it on the rock and promised that the gates of hell would not prevail against it. He called it "my Church" (Mt. 16: 18). He is its head and the source of its life. In the second place, He knows it intimately. In each of the seven letters He begins "I know". "I know your works, your toil, your patient endurance", He says. "I know your tribulation and your poverty". "I know where you dwell". "I know . . . your love and faith and service" (2: 2, 9, 13, 19). He is walking among the lampstands, patrolling and supervising His churches. He is the chief pastor, the chief bishop. Then what is His view of His Church? In each of the seven letters which follow, the risen Christ lays emphasis, either in rebuke or in commendation, on one particular characteristic of an ideal church. Put together, these characteristics constitute the seven marks of a true and living church. They tell us what Christ thinks of His Church, both as it is and as it should be. To a study of these letters we must now proceed.

2

THE LETTER TO EPHESUS: LOVE
(Rev. 2: 1-7)

TO the angel of the church in Ephesus write: "The words of him who holds the seven stars in his right hand, who walks among the seven golden lampstands. I know your works, your toil and your patient endurance, and how you cannot bear evil men but have tested those who call themselves apostles but are not, and found them to be false; I know you are enduring patiently and bearing up for my name's sake, and you have not grown weary. But I have this against you, that you have abandoned the love you had at first. Remember then from what you have fallen, repent and do the works you did at first. If not, I will come to you and remove your lampstand from its place, unless you repent. Yet this you have, you hate the works of the Nicolaitans, which I also hate. He who has an ear, let him hear what the Spirit says to the churches. To him who conquers I will grant to eat of the tree of life, which is in the paradise of God."

The first of the seven letters is addressed to the church in Ephesus, if for no better reason because it was nearer to the island of Patmos than the other six cities. A straight sail of sixty miles would bring the bearer of the letter to the port of Ephesus at the mouth of the River Cayster. But Ephesus was more than the nearest city to Patmos. It had a distinction of its own. Its citizens liked to call it "the metropolis of Asia", and indeed it was the capital of the Roman Province. It was also a prosperous business centre, particularly because it was situated on the trade route from Rome to the east. Its magnificent Ionic temple in honour of Diana, or Artemis, was acknowledged as one of the seven wonders of the world.

The apostle Paul had been frustrated in his attempt to visit Ephesus when outward bound on his second missionary journey. We do not know the circumstances, but in Luke's language he was "forbidden by the Holy Spirit to speak the word in Asia" (Acts 16: 6). However, on his return journey he paid Ephesus a brief visit and evidently recognized its strategic importance so clearly that he went straight there on his third journey and spent about two and a half years in the city. He gave public lectures and visited people privately in their homes, and the gospel spread throughout the whole neighbourhood. In the end a riot broke out over the drop in sales of the silver models of Diana's temple. The uproar is vividly described by Luke in Acts 19. Paul had to leave the town, but he left Timothy behind, to supervise the growing work and to guard the truth of the gospel. He later wrote from his first imprisonment in Rome his letter to the Ephesian church, and later still his two letters to Timothy. According to an early tradition St. John replaced Timothy towards the end of the first century as leader of the Ephesian church, and probably wrote his first epistle for them. Now John is in exile for the truth, but is given the opportunity of writing to his beloved church an epistle which is dictated to him by Jesus Christ.

(1) THE LETTER BEGINS WITH A COMMENDATION

In each of the seven letters Jesus Christ passes a moral judgment upon the church concerned. To the church in Smyrna He gives unmixed praise, but to the church in Laodicea He expresses unrelieved condemnation. The Philadelphian church is more praised than blamed and the church in Sardis more blamed than praised, while in the letters to Pergamum and

Thyatira and this first one to Ephesus, approval and disapproval are fairly evenly balanced.

It is clear that the risen Lord is in a position to evaluate the condition of each church and to commend or condemn them, for He knows their state with perfect accuracy. We have already seen that every letter is introduced by the statement "I know". Of course He knows. As He says here, it is He *who holds the seven stars in His right hand, who walks among the seven golden lampstands* (v. 1). The claim is even stronger here than the earlier one in the first chapter. He not only "has" the stars; He "holds" them. He not only stands in the midst of the lampstands; He "walks among" them. He is the divine overseer of the churches. Did He not say "where two or three are gathered in my name, there am I in the midst of them" (Mt. 18: 20)? Christ visits His people. He dwells with them. He walks among them. He inspects them. He knows them.

The church at Ephesus exhibited three virtues which Jesus Christ could commend without qualification.

(i) Their toil. *I know your works*, He says and immediately adds by way of explanation, *your toil*. The Greek word is well translated in the Revised Standard Version. It means "diligent labour", and even according to Archbishop R. C. Trench "labour unto weariness" or "strenuous and exhausting labour" (*Commentary on the Epistles to the Seven Churches in Asia*, pp. 71 and 76). It is not just work, but hard work. The Ephesian church was an active church, busy in the service of God and men. Perhaps the church of Ephesus had its "Guild of Help" or "Active Service League". Its members were fully occupied, entertaining the lonely and nursing the sick, teaching the young and visiting the aged. No doubt some gave hours of their time to making and mending, sewing and knitting for the church. Others spent their leisure hours writing and cooking and cleaning and organizing. The church of Ephesus was a veritable beehive of industry. Their toil was famous. Every member was doing something for Christ. They were diligent, and conscientious.

(ii) Their endurance. Evidently the Christians in Ephesus had been exposed to some fierce local opposition. Ephesus was a meeting place of many religions. It was one of the great centres of emperor worship in the province. Some of its inhabitants practised magical arts from the orient, while everybody had a profound reverence for the great Diana of the Ephesians, the mother goddess of Asia, on account of whom the city had been put in a ferment through St. Paul's preaching. Craftsmen feared for their sales of silver shrines, and their vested interests led them to oppose Paul violently. Paul had left Ephesus and died long ago, but the unpopularity of Christians still lingered. Christians in Ephesus knew what it was to be hated, to be snubbed in public and maligned in private. Some found business hard, since they were losing customers. Others found shopping a problem as a number of tradesmen would not sell to Christians. John was to describe later in his book how through the influence of the "false prophet" (or "beast from the earth") no one could buy or sell unless he bore on him the mark of the beast (13: 17). This probably means that those who would not indulge in the popular worship of the emperor (or perhaps of Diana) were boycotted. There had even perhaps been physical violence to endure, as well as social ostracism.

Nevertheless, despite all this tribulation, the Ephesians had not thrown their Christianity overboard. They were firm and unswerving in their allegiance to Jesus Christ. *I know . . . your patient endurance* (v. 2), He says to them in this letter.

(iii) Their orthodoxy. This was their third virtue which Christ could unreservedly praise. Ephesus had been visited by some self-styled apostles, called (either by themselves, by others or by John) *Nicolaitans* (v. 6). Exactly who they were and what they taught it is hard to say with any dogmatism. Some of the early Fathers believed they were disciples of Nicolaus, the "proselyte of Antioch" who is mentioned in Acts 6: 5 as one of the seven chosen to help the apostles in practical ministry. This may or may not be so. It is enough here to know that their teaching was seriously mistaken, especially in its condonation of immorality. Trench thinks the name is symbolical, like the rest of the names in the Revelation, and points out that the Greek word Nikolaos means "Destroyer of the People", an apt epithet for this baneful sect. They were spreading their evil doctrines throughout the churches of Asia. They are mentioned again by name in the letter to Pergamum, where we shall consider their teaching in greater detail, and probably by implication in the letters to Thyatira and Sardis as well.

Paul had warned the elders of the Ephesian church that such an invasion of heretical teachers would take place. Returning to Palestine at the end of his third missionary journey, his ship put in at Miletus, thirty-five miles away, and he sent for them to come to him. In his charge to them, he said: "I know that after my departure fierce wolves will come in among you, not sparing the flock; and from among your own selves will arise men speaking perverse things, to draw away the disciples after them." Now the wolves had come. Ravenous beasts had got into the sheepfold. False prophets were insinuating their dark and dangerous doctrines among the elect. What did the Ephesian Christians do in this situation? At first they listened. They could not tell whether the teaching of the Nicolaitans was from man, from Satan or from God until they had given it a fair hearing. But as they heard it, they sifted it. They "tested the spirits", to see whether they were from God (1 Jn. 4: 1). They "proved all things", desiring to hold fast only what was good, and to abstain from every form of evil (1 Thess. 5: 21, 22). No doubt they thought and prayed and discussed. They will also have searched the scriptures and compared the teaching of these vaunted apostles with the primitive apostolic doctrine which they had received. Then after an honest hearing and a careful testing they absolutely rejected the Nicolaitans' message.

The*y tested those who call themselves apostles but are not, and found them to be false* (v. 2). It was not just the belief of the Nicolaitans which was faulty, but their behaviour. Jesus Himself had said that a prophet could be known by his works as a tree is told by its fruit. So the Ephesians examined the works of the Nicolaitans and came to detest them. *This you have*, said the risen Jesus in His commendation, *you hate the works of the Nicolaitans, which I also hate* (v. 6). The Ephesians had not been deceived. They possessed the rare gift of discernment. They were discriminating. Their orthodoxy was unimpaired. They were not so stupid as to suppose that Christian charity can tolerate such false apostles. Love embraces neither error nor evil. I trust they did not hate the Nicolaitans; but they hated their works, and utterly repudiated them. There is a deliberate contrast in the statement that although they could *bear* trials and tribulations for the sake of Christ's name (v. 3), they could not *bear* the company of these evil men (v. 2). A few years later this church was still renowned for its doctrinal purity. Bishop Ignatius of Antioch wrote to them: "ye all live according to truth and no heresy hath a home among you; nay, ye do not so much as listen to anyone if he speak of aught else save concerning Jesus Christ in truth" (Quoted by Prof. W. M. Ramsay, *The Letters to the Seven Churches of Asia*, p. 241).

What a splendid church was the church of Ephesus! It appeared to be a model church in every way. Its members were busy in their service, patient in their sufferings, and orthodox in their belief. What more could be asked of them? Only one thing was lacking, and Jesus Christ lays His finger gently on it. In doing so, He is obliged to turn from commendation to complaint.

(2) THE LETTER CONTINUES WITH A COMPLAINT

But I have this against you, that you have abandoned the love you had at first (v. 4). They had left their first love. They had fallen from the early heights of devotion to Christ which they had climbed. They had descended to the plains of mediocrity. In a word, they were backsliders. Did not Jesus Himself prophesy that when wickedness multiplies, "most men's love will grow cold" (Mt. 24: 12)? Certainly the hearts of the Ephesian Christians had chilled.

The words of Christ's complaint do not themselves make clear whether the first love which they had abandoned was love for Himself or for their fellowmen, but the analogy with the Old Testament makes the former almost certain.

God often likened Israel to His bride and Himself to her husband. He had set His love upon her. She was "at the age for love" (Ezek. 16: 8), so He had taken her to Himself. He had plighted His troth to her and entered into a covenant with her. But alas! she began to flirt with other lovers, the gods of the land of Canaan. She played the harlot with them. She became unfaithful and forsook her true husband. So Jeremiah proclaimed the word of the Lord in the hearing of the inhabitants of Jerusalem: "I remember the devotion of your youth, your love as a bride, how you followed me in the wilderness, in a land not sown" (2: 2).

In the New Testament the new Israel (which is the Christian Church) is represented as married to Christ as the old Israel was married to Jehovah. "I betrothed you to Christ", wrote St. Paul to the Corinthians, "to present you as a pure bride to her one husband. But I am afraid that as the serpent deceived Eve by his cunning, your thoughts will be led astray from a sincere and pure devotion to Christ" (2 Cor. 11: 2, 3). This very tendency was apparent at Ephesus, and the Heavenly Bridegroom complains *I have this against you: that you have abandoned the love you had at first.* Their first flush of ecstasy had passed. Their early devotion to Christ had cooled. They had been in love with Him, but they had fallen out of love.

So the Bridegroom seeks to woo His bride back, back to her first love. With the same tenderness that Jehovah showed to fickle, adulterous Israel, the Lord Jesus appeals to His Church to return to Him. The prophet Hosea, who had learned through the agony of his own wife's unfaithfulness how unquenchable

is the love of God, conveyed God's word to the old Israel:
"Behold, I will allure her, and bring her into the wilderness, and
speak tenderly to her . . . and there she shall answer as in the
days of her youth, as at the time when she came out of the land
of Egypt. And in that day . . . you will call me 'My
husband' . . .". Again, "I will betroth you to me for ever; I
will betroth you to me in righteousness and in justice, in steadfast love, and in mercy. I will betroth you to me in faithfulness;
and you shall know the Lord" (Hos. 2: 14-16, 19-20).

The Divine Lover still sorrows when His love is unrequited,
and pines for our continuing, deepening, maturing adoration.
Love, then, is the first mark of a true and living church. Indeed,
it is not a living church at all unless it is a loving church. The
Christian life is essentially a love-relationship to Jesus Christ.
"Jesus captured me", wrote Prebendary Wilson Carlile, founder
and "chief" of the Church Army. "For me to know Jesus is a
love affair" (*Yours in the Fight* by A. E. Reffold, p. 15).

Without this love, the Church's work is lifeless. It is significant
that St. Paul ended his epistle to the Ephesians with a special
prayer for all those "who love our Lord Jesus Christ with love
undying" (6: 24). Some thirty years had passed since then. A
new generation had arisen in the Ephesian church, which did
not heed this warning. Their love was faltering, weakening,
dying. The tide of devotion had turned and was ebbing fast.
They toiled with vigour, but not with love. They endured with
fortitude but without love. They tested their teachers with
orthodoxy, but had no love in their hearts.

However, toil becomes drudgery if it is not a labour of love.
Jacob could work seven years for the hand of Rachel only
because he loved her, and the seven years "seemed to him but
a few days because of the love he had for her" (Gen. 29: 20).
The endurance of suffering can be hard and bitter if it is not
softened and sweetened by love. It is one thing to grit the teeth
and clench the fists with Stoical indifference, and quite another
to smile in the face of adversity with Christian love. As for

orthodoxy, it is cold and dead and grim without the warmth and life and beauty with which love invests it. The Ephesians even hated the evil deeds and words of the Nicolaitans, so unimpeachable was their theological correctness, but to hate error and evil is not the same as to love Jesus Christ.

Again and again the New Testament reiterates its emphasis on the pre-eminence of love. In Professor Henry Drummond's famous phrase it is "the greatest thing in the world". Indeed, it is the greatest thing in the universe. The first and great commandment is to love both God and man. So, to love is to fulfil the law. Love is itself the "royal law". Love is greater than knowledge, asserts Paul in his first letter to the Corinthians, because whereas knowledge puffs up, love builds up. Knowledge can merely inflate the clever man with wind, while love develops solid character. Besides, knowledge concerns things, whereas love concerns persons, including the person of God; and the knowledge of a doctrine is a one-sided, static affair, while love is reciprocal and growing (8: 1-3). Love is greater even than faith and hope, writes the great apostle of faith and hope, who elsewhere declares that the sinner is justified by faith only and so rejoices in hope of seeing and sharing the glory of God. For love is everlasting and indestructible. Prophecy, knowledge and the gift of tongues are only temporary, but "love never ends". "So faith, hope, love abide, these three; but the greatest of these is love" (1 Cor. 13).

Some people may be disposed to think that the particular love for Christ, which He desired and the church of Ephesus lacked, is an unpractical and abstract sentiment. On the contrary, true love leads to the most concrete and wholesome results. After listing many Christian qualities in one of his epistles, Paul concludes: "Above all these put on love, which binds everything together in perfect harmony" (Col. 3: 14). Love can and should pervade all our thoughts, words and deeds. It adds lustre to all that it touches and zest to all that it inspires. Here are some of its products.

(i) A deeper worship. It is the duty of man to worship God, of the creature to worship his Creator, but the duty is barren without love. If the worship of the Church is to be more than lip-service, it must spring from hearts that love God. True worship is the response of man's whole personality to God's whole revelation, and if God has spoken and acted in Christ for our redemption, the most prominent quality of our response will be love. I expect the worship of the church of Ephesus was almost dead. The singing had become drab and uninspired, and the prayers were scarcely better than heathen incantations. There was form but no spirit. There was no life because there was no love. What was true of the public worship of the Ephesian Christians was true no doubt of their private devotions also. Only love can save private prayer and Bible reading from degenerating into a mechanical routine. Only if we love Christ, shall we ardently desire every day to spend an unhurried time sitting at His feet, seeking His face and listening to His word.

(ii) A prompter obedience. To obey is another certain consequence of love. We must remember that what the Bible means by love is not primarily an emotion. It is more loyalty than affection, and comes under the control of the will rather than of the emotions. It is the purposeful commitment of one person to another person, in which the lover sets his beloved's will and welfare before his own. So Jesus made obedience the test of love. "If you love me", He said, "you will keep my commandments", and "he who has my commandments and keeps them, he it is who loves me", and again, "If a man loves me, he will keep my word" (Jn. 14: 15, 21, 23). How dare we claim to love Christ if we disobey Him? Truly to love Him is to seek His pleasure, and to seek His pleasure is to do His will. The church which loves is a church which obeys.

(iii) A more sacrificial love for others. This also will follow if we return to our first love for Christ. Love for Christ is not a pietistic experience indulged in the private sanctuary of the heart, which has no effect upon our life in the world. No. "If any one says, 'I love God', and hates his brother, he is a liar; for he who does not love his brother whom he has seen, cannot love God whom he has not seen. And this commandment we have from Him, that he who loves God should love his brother also" (1 Jn. 4: 20, 21). Moreover, the Christian's love for his neighbour is no more unpractical than his love for God. It concerns action more than affection. Its essence is self-sacrifice. The pagan notion of love is the desire to get; the Christian notion is the desire to give. Genuine love longs to enrich its object, not to possess it. So love expresses itself in a thousand ways of practical and humble service. "If any one has the world's goods and sees his brother in need, yet closes his heart against him, how does God's love abide in him? Little children, let us not love in word or speech but in deed and in truth" (1 Jn. 3: 17, 18).

So we come back in thought to Ephesus, the church that toiled and endured and believed the truth, but the church which did not love.

(3) THE LETTER CONCLUDES WITH A COMMAND

Jesus Christ is not content to leave the church of Ephesus, nor any church, wandering in the deserts of lovelessness. He will recall her to her senses. He will bring her back to the oases of love. So he issues to the Ephesian Church three terse words of command (v. 5).

First, the church is commanded to remember its former condition. *Remember then from what you have fallen.* Memory is a precious gift. To look back can be sinful; but it can also be sensible. To look back with lustful eyes, as Lot's wife did, to the sins of Sodom from which we have been delivered, is to court disaster. To look back wistfully to the easy-going comforts of the world once we have put our hand to the plough, is to be unfit for the Kingdom of God. But to look back along the way that God has led us is the least that gratitude bids us do, and to look back to the spiritual heights which once by the grace of God we occupied, is to take the first step along the road of repentance. We must not live in the past. But to recall it, and to compare what we are with what we were, is a salutary, and may be a disturbing, experience.

Secondly, the church is commanded to *repent*. Now, repentance is a change of mind leading to a change of direction. It is resolutely and completely to turn one's back on all known sin. Jesus Christ does not advocate the conjuring up of an emotional experience. He does not urge the Ephesian Christians to feel bad about their sins. It is not what they feel about them which matters, so much as what they do about them. They must not wait till they feel sorry. The fact is they have sinned, and they must turn from their sin in repentance. There is no need to wait. They must first recall what has been good in their past and then reject what has been wrong. Let them confess their loss of love and give it up. How sane and matter-of-fact is this word of Christ! So many of us admit and bemoan our present state, but wait for some vague emotional upheaval to set us right. We are like children who fall in a puddle and sit in the mud waiting for someone to pick them up. But their duty is to get up at once. So is ours, just as soon as we are conscious of any sin.

Thirdly, the church is commanded to resume its former state. *Do the works you did at first.* Again, there is no waiting. There is no suggestion that, having fallen out of love with Christ, they must delay until they have fallen in love with Him again. Having abandoned their first love, they must go back to it. By God's grace it is in their power to do so. They have fallen from the heights of love; let them take them by storm again. They have lost what once they had; they must recapture it. "Renew your early devotion to me", says Christ; "resume the works you used to do." The works will be the same as they were during the intervening period of lovelessness, or similar. But there will be a new vigour in the doing of them, a new singleness of mind and purity of motive, a new secret of joyful perseverance

in the face of many trials, and a new care even for those whose
false words and evil deeds the Ephesians would continue rightly
to hate. Love will cause a transformation scene on the stage of
Ephesus.

Jesus Christ does not only issue commands; He enforces them
with strong arguments, and with these this brief epistle closes. He
adds to His instruction a solemn warning and a gracious promise.

He warns them that if they disobey His commands, and do
not repent, their church's existence will be ignominiously
terminated. *I will come to you and remove your lampstand from its
place, unless you repent* (v. 5). No church has a secure and permanent place in the world. It is continously on trial. If we can
judge from the letter which Bishop Ignatius of Antioch wrote
to the Ephesian church at the beginning of the second century,
it rallied after Christ's appeal. Ignatius describes it in glowing
terms. But later it lapsed again, and by the Middle Ages its
Christian testimony had been obliterated. "The little railway
station and hotel and few poor dwelling houses of Ayasaluk,
which now command the ruins of the city, are eloquent of the
doom which has overtaken both Ephesus and its church" (H. B.
Swete, *The Apocalypse of St. John:* p. 27). Otherwise, there is
nothing but rubble and a bog. A traveller visiting the village
"found only three Christians there", writes Trench (p. 81) "and
these sunken in such ignorance and apathy as scarcely to have
heard the names of St. Paul or St. John."

Christ's warning to Ephesus is just as appropriate to us today.
Our own church's light will be extinguished if we stubbornly
persevere in our refusal to love Christ. The church has no light
without love. Only when its love burns can its light shine.
Many churches all over the world today have ceased truly to
exist. Their buildings remain intact, their ministers minister
and their congregations congregate, but their lampstand has
been removed. The church is plunged in darkness. No glimmer
of light radiates from it. It has no light, because it has no love.
Let us heed this warning before it is too late.

To this warning for the impenitent, Christ adds a promise to the penitent. *To him who conquers I will grant to eat of the tree of life, which is in the paradise of God* (v. 7). Each of the seven letters ends with a promise to the conqueror, to the person, that is, who obeys the message of the letter and overcomes in the conflict with evil. The promise in this case is particularly apt. It offers free access to the tree of life in God's paradise, whose fruit was previously forbidden to man. This means the enjoyment of eternal life in heaven. But what is eternal life if it is not to know and love God and His Son Jesus Christ (Jn. 17: 3)? and what is heaven but the abode of love? For heaven is where God is, and God is love. So the reward of love is more love in the perfect communion of heaven.

No hint is given in this letter as to how love may be quickened, but John tells us the way in his first general epistle. "We love", he writes, "because He first loved us" (1 Jn. 4: 19). This prior love of God took Christ to the cross to die for the sins of the world. There He gave Himself for us with the absolute self-giving of love, as He bore our sins in His own body. "By this we know love, that He laid down His life for us" (1 Jn. 3: 16). The cross is the blazing fire at which the flame of our love is kindled, but we have to get near enough to it for its sparks to fall on us.

So the Church today, like the church of Ephesus, has a work to be done, a fight to be fought and a creed to be championed. But above all it has a Person to be loved, with the love we had for Him at first, a "love undying".

A PRAYER

O God, who hast prepared for them that love Thee such good things as pass man's understanding; pour into our hearts such love toward Thee, that we, loving Thee above all things, may obtain Thy promises, which exceed all that we can desire, through Jesus Christ our Lord.

(*Collect for Trinity* VI).

3

THE LETTER TO SMYRNA: SUFFERING
(Rev. 2: 8-11)

*A*ND to the angel of the church in Smyrna write: "The words of
the first and the last, who died and came to life. I know your
tribulation and your poverty (but you are rich) and the slander of
those who say that they are Jews and are not, but are a synagogue of
Satan. Do not fear what you are about to suffer. Behold, the devil
is about to throw some of you into prison, that you may be tested, and
for ten days you will have tribulation. Be faithful unto death, and I
will give you the crown of life. He who has an ear, let him hear what
the Spirit says to the churches. He who conquers shall not be hurt by
the second death."*

If the first mark of a true and living church is love, the second
is suffering. The one is naturally consequent on the other. A
willingness to suffer proves the genuineness of love. We are
willing to suffer for those we love. Evidently Christians in
Smyrna had not lost their pristine love for Christ, as had the
Christians in Ephesus, for they were prepared to suffer for Him.
Like Peter and John, they were "rejoicing that they were counted
worthy to suffer dishonour for the (*sc.* Christ's) name"
(Acts 5: 41).

The town of Smyrna is situated about thirty-five miles up
coast from, and almost due north of, Ephesus. It was the next
city the postman would reach on his circular tour of the seven
churches. Commentators describe it as the most splendid of the

seven cities. It boastfully regarded itself as the "pride of Asia" and was sensitive to the rivalry of Ephesus. A fine road gave it access to the interior, and its excellent natural harbour commanded a flourishing export trade. According to Archdeacon R. H. Charles, it was then, and has remained ever since, "one of the most prosperous cities of Asia Minor" (*The International Critical Commentary on the Revelation*, p. 55).

In the city of Smyrna was the church of Smyrna. We do not know when it was founded. It is mentioned neither in the Acts nor in the New Testament epistles, although an early tradition states that the apostle Paul visited the town on his way to Ephesus at the beginning of his third missionary tour.

What was the ascended Lord's message to His servants in Smyrna?

(1) THE SUFFERINGS THEY ENDURED FOR CHRIST

The Smyrnaean church was a suffering church, and this epistle is exclusively devoted to an account of their past and present sufferings, a warning of severer trials yet to come, and encouragements to them to endure. We will begin with the sufferings. The comforts we can consider later.

I know your tribulation (v. 9). Clearly their tribulation was persecution. The church of Smyrna was up against it. The enemies of the faith were aggressive and cruel. It was a dangerous thing to be a Christian in Smyrna. There was no knowing what might happen to you.

The causes of the persecution are not given, but it is not difficult to reconstruct the situation. Already in 195 B.C. a temple to Dea Roma, Rome personified as a goddess, had been built and dedicated in Smyrna, and the city had acquired a reputation for its patriotic loyalty to the Empire. Round about the year A.D. 25 many Asian cities were competing with one another for the coveted favour of erecting a temple to the Emperor Tiberius, and the privilege was granted to Smyrna alone.

Evidently then the cult of Empire and Emperor, of Rome and Rome's Caesar, was a matter of great pride in Smyrna. Did the Christians refuse to sprinkle incense on the fire which burned before the emperor's bust? Of course they did. To do so would be idolatry. They could not call Caesar Lord when Jesus was their Lord. But their unwillingness to conform was interpreted by the common people as a disgraceful and even treacherous lack of patriotism.

It is plain too from this epistle that the popular antagonism to the Christians for their refusal to take part in emperor worship was fanned into flame by the local Jewish population. They were themselves exempt from all sacrificial obligations and exploited their privilege to harry the hated Nazarenes. They were no doubt suspect for their own refusal to sacrifice. So they curried favour with the authorities and the people by urging the Christians to sacrifice and vilifying them if they would not. This Jewish opposition, so bitter and vociferous in demanding from Pilate the crucifixion of Jesus, had dogged the footsteps of Paul throughout his missionary expeditions. It was the Jews who were jealous of the multitudes when they thronged to hear him in Pisidian Antioch and who incited some of the leading men and women of the city to drive out him and Barnabas. They pursued him to Iconium, and on to Lystra, where they persuaded the people to stone him and nearly killed him. In Thessalonica they caused a riot and in Corinth they so vigorously opposed the gospel that Paul "shook out his garments and said to them 'Your blood be upon your heads! I am innocent. From now on I will go to the Gentiles'." When he was back in Jerusalem, they arrested him in the temple and nearly killed him. When this attempt failed, they did their best by secret plots and public accusations to have him put to death. The Book of Acts ends with him in Rome still disputing with them and condemning them for being culpably blind and deaf. He even described them as those "who killed both the Lord Jesus and the prophets, and drove us out, and displease God and oppose all men by hindering us from speaking to the Gentiles that they may be saved" (Acts 13: 45, 50; 14: 2, 5, 19; 17: 5-7; 18: 5, 6; 21: 27; 25: 12; 28: 17-28; 1 Thess. 2: 14-16).

This fanatical Jewish hostility to Christians was seen in the middle of the second century A.D. when in this same town of Smyrna its saintly Bishop Polycarp was martyred. A description of this will be given later, but it may be mentioned now that it was the voice of the Jews which cried loudest that he should be thrown to the lions; and when the order was finally given for him to be burned alive, the most diligent of the crowd to fetch faggots for the fatal wood-pile were Jews.

So much for the causes of persecution in Smyrna. What form did the tribulation take? How did the Christians suffer? Four trials are mentioned.

(i) Poverty. *I know your poverty* (v. 9), Christ says. It is at first most surprising that in the midst of wealthy and prosperous Smyrna any of its citizens should have been poor. It may be that the Christians in Smyrna belonged to the lower ranks of society. We know that in those days "not many . . . were wise according to worldly standards, not many were powerful, not many were of noble birth" (1 Cor. 1: 26). It may be too that in the Christians' unselfish love for the underprivileged, they had contributed generously to their needs and like the Macedonians "their extreme poverty . . . overflowed in a wealth of liberality" (2 Cor. 8: 2). But neither of these factors would explain why their poverty was part of their "tribulation". It is more probable that in their resolve to go straight in business, they renounced shady methods and thereby missed some of the easy profits which went to others less scrupulous than themselves. Or again, no doubt many Jews and pagans would not trade with them when they knew they were Christians. They were cold-shouldered. It was not always easy for them to find employment. It is even possible that some of the Smyrna Christians had had their homes pillaged. To them it might have been written: "you joyfully accepted the plundering of your property, since you knew that you yourselves had a better possession and an abiding one" (Heb. 10: 34). Make no mistake: it does not always pay to be a Christian. Nor is honesty by any means always the best policy, if material gain is your ambition. Poverty has often been part of the cost of Christian discipleship.

(ii) Slander. *I know . . . the slander of those who say that they are Jews and are not* (v. 9). Jewish tongues were wagging busily. False rumours were circulating. Minds were being poisoned. Truly no man can tame the tongue; it is a deadly evil. And slander is never easy to bear. "La calomnie, monsieur? Vous ne savez guère ce que vous dédaignez. . . ." (*Le Barbier de Séville*, Act 2, Scene 8, by Beaumarchais). The foes of Christ were misrepresenting His people, speaking evil against them, "blaspheming" them (for that is what the Greek word is). Christ here calls them *a synagogue* not of the Lord but *of Satan* (v. 9, cf. 3: 9). They learned their ways from their master who is later called "the devil" (v. 10), which means "the accuser", "the slanderer". Christ had called him "a liar and the father of lies" (Jn. 8: 44), and his followers share his distaste for the truth. They were spreading untrue, unkind remarks behind the Christians' backs. Gossip has a strange fascination for all of us. As the Book of Proverbs says: "The words of a whisperer are like delicious morsels; they go down into the inner parts of the body" (26: 22). And the unbelievers of Smyrna fully indulged their hunger for these succulent dainties. But the Christians were deeply wounded by their abuse. It was painful to be so misunderstood and caricatured. Still, I have no doubt that they followed in the steps of their lowly Master, of whom it is written: "When He was reviled, He did not revile in return; when He suffered, He did not threaten; but He trusted to Him who judges justly" (1 Pet. 2: 23).

Poverty and slander were the two experiences of tribulation which the church of Smyrna was already enduring. But there was more and worse to come. To this Christ now refers and tells them: *Do not fear what you are about to suffer* (v. 10).

(iii) Prison. *Behold, the devil is about to throw some of you into prison.* The early apostles, and the apostle Paul, had seen the inside of many prisons. The cells of Jerusalem and Caesarea, of Philippi and Rome, had been sanctified by the prayers and praises of Christian believers. Their darkness had been illumined by the light of God's word, and their smells relieved by the fragrance of Christ's presence. It was in Neuchâtel prison in Switzerland that more recently the Maréchale, daughter of William Booth, the founder of the Salvation Army, wrote one of her well-known hymns:

> Best-beloved of my soul,
>   I am here alone with Thee;
> And my prison is a heaven
>   Since Thou sharest it with me.

(iv) Death. *Be faithful unto death* (v. 10). *Unto* here means not "until" but "even unto" (Dean H. Alford in the Greek Testament *ad loc.*). Christ's exhortation to these persecuted believers is to be faithful "to the extent of being ready to die for my sake" (Swete p. 32). Opposition to the gospel was so fierce that martyrdom appeared a real and solemn possibility. Indeed, one of the best-known Christian martyrs of all ages was a native of Smyrna. Reference has already been made to him in this chapter. Polycarp was in all probability already a member of the church of Smyrna at the time this letter was written. Some have even argued that he was already its chief minister, since both Tertullian and Irenaeus say that he was consecrated Bishop of Smyrna by St. John himself. At all events, he will have read this letter and no doubt pondered on its message. Perhaps it was a source of strength to him when his hour of trial came. This is what happened.

It was 22 February, probably in the year A.D 156. The venerable bishop, who had fled from the city at the entreaty of his congregation, was tracked down to his hiding-place. He made no attempt to flee. Instead, he offered food and drink to his captors and asked permission to retire for prayer, which he did for two hours. Then, as they drove into the city, the officer in charge urged him to recant. "What harm can it do", he asked, "to sacrifice to the emperor?" Polycarp refused. On arrival, he was roughly pushed out of the carriage, and brought before the proconsul in the amphitheatre, who addressed him: "Have respect to your old age . . . Swear by the genius of Caesar . . .". And again, "Swear, and I will release you; revile the Christ". To which Polycarp replied: "Eighty and six years have I served Him, and He has done me no wrong; how then can I blaspheme my King who saved me?" The Proconsul persisted: "Swear by the genius of Caesar. . . . I have wild beasts; if you will not change your mind, I will throw you to them . . .". "Bid them be brought . . .". "As you despise the beasts, unless you change your mind, I make you to be destroyed by fire". Infuriated Jews and Gentiles gathered wood for the pile. Polycarp stood by the stake, asking not to be fastened to it, and prayed "O Lord, Almighty God, the Father of Thy beloved Son Jesus Christ, through whom we have received a knowledge of Thee. . . . I thank Thee that Thou hast thought me worthy, this day and this hour, to share the cup of Thy Christ among the number of Thy witnesses!" The fire was kindled, but as the wind drove the flames away from him and prolonged his agony, a soldier's sword put an end to his misery. (Quotations from the Epistle of the Church of Smyrna, translated mostly by B. Jackson in *Documents Illustrative of the History of the Christian Church*, edited by B. J. Kidd.)

This call to suffer, here addressed to the church of Smyrna, is timeless in its application. In the New Testament suffering is an indispensable mark of every true Christian and church, and the inevitability of the world's persecution is stressed over and over again. Among the beatitudes in which Christ pronounces blessed the meek and the merciful, mourners and peacemakers, the poor in spirit and the pure in heart, He added His final blessing to those who are persecuted for righteousness' sake. "Blessed are you when men shall revile you and persecute you and utter all kinds of evil against you falsely on my account. Rejoice and be glad, for your reward is great in heaven, for so men persecuted the prophets who were before you."—To this beatitude Christ appended a complementary woe when He said: "Woe to you, when all men speak well of you, for so their fathers did to the false prophets" (Mt. 5: 10-12; Lk. 6: 26). Not once but many times this theme recurred in His teaching. "If the world hates you, know that it has hated me before it hated you. . . . Remember the word that I said to you. 'A servant is not greater than his Master.' If they persecuted me, they will persecute you . . .". "In the world you have tribulation" (Jn. 15: 18, 20; 16: 33). Jesus Himself experienced the very same poverty and slander, arrest and death, of which He now writes to the church of Smyrna.

What Christ taught, the New Testament apostles both echoed in their writings and endured in their ministries. The catalogue of his sufferings included by St. Paul in his second letter to the Corinthians makes us lesser mortals tremble. He was imprisoned, flogged and shipwrecked; he braved the dangers of travel by sea, river and land, and was exposed to the savagery of inumerable enemies (11: 23-27). No wonder he could write to Timothy: "all who desire to live a godly life in Christ Jesus will be persecuted" (2 Tim. 3: 12), and to the Philippians: "It has been granted to you that for the sake of Christ you should not only believe in Him but also suffer for His sake" (1: 29). It is given to every Christian to believe in Christ, and to every Christian to suffer for Christ. Faith and suffering are linked together as twin Christian privileges.

Many Christian writers have recognized in more recent days that suffering is the hallmark of the genuine church. Dietrich Bonhoeffer, the Lutheran pastor who was hanged by direct order of Himmler in the Flossenburg concentration camp on 9 April 1945, wrote: "Suffering then is the badge of the true

Christian. The disciple is not above his master. . . . Luther reckoned suffering among the marks of the true church, and one of the memoranda drawn up in preparation for the Augsburg Confession similarly defines the Church as the community of those 'who are persecuted and martyred for the gospel's sake'. . . . Discipleship means allegiance to the suffering Christ, and it is therefore not at all surprising that Christians should be called upon to suffer. . . ." (*The Cost of Discipleship*, 1937, p. 74).

Down the Christian centuries this has proved to be true, until in our own day in Kenya and in Soviet lands, in China and Colombia and South Africa, Christian people have suffered and are suffering for their faith.

What about ourselves? We are men of flesh. We shrink from suffering. But what about us? Take England and the Church of England. We who are Christians of the Church of England do not suffer much. The ugly truth is that we tend to avoid suffering by compromise. Our moral standards are often not noticeably higher than the standards of the world. Our lives do not challenge and rebuke unbelievers by their integrity or purity or love. The world sees in us nothing to hate. As for the Church, in many places the world hardly notices it. It makes little impact on society; its discipline is in many ways lax and its commitment halfhearted. By "it" I mean "we", and by "its", "our". We are seldom bold to rebuke vice. We mind our own business lest anyone should be offended. We hold our tongue so that nobody is embarrassed. We tread more delicately than Agag in our anxiety not to step on anybody's corns. We are respectable, conventional, inoffensive and ineffective. Of course there are notable exceptions to this generalization; but it remains substantially true for the Church of England in England.

Two obvious examples come to my mind. The first concerns the message we preach. The most recent statistics suggest that although a large percentage of our country's population believe in God only about ten per cent regularly attend any place of worship. In other words, vast multitudes of our nation are ignorant of the saving truths of the Christian gospel. Why? Because they have never heard them. Why? Because they are seldom preached. Why? Because they are unpopular. Such facts of the Biblical revelation as the universal sin of man, the wrath of God against sin, the atoning death of Jesus Christ, justification by faith only, the need for conversion and the sanctifying work of the Holy Spirit are seldom heard from our pulpits today and if heard are often so travestied as to be almost unrecognizable. The fear of man has ensnared us. We trim our sails to the prevailing theological wind. We dilute the gospel so as to render it supposedly more palatable. We love the praise of men more than the praise of God. We escape suffering by compromise.

The second example which occurs to me concerns not the message we preach but the discipline we administer. Take the indiscriminate baptism of infants. Ever since the Emperor Constantine embraced the Christian faith and Christianity ceased to be a *religio illicita* the world has flooded the Church. Our ranks are filled with baptized unbelievers. It has become respectable to have a Christian name. All manner of wild and idle superstitions surround the ordinance of baptism. But, leaving aside altogether the question of the propriety of baptizing infants, is it right to baptize them indiscriminately? Can it ever be justifiable to baptize into Christ and His Church children who have neither parents nor godparents who profess the Christian faith? Can we really dare to put into adult lips, on behalf of a child, solemn declarations of Christian repentance, faith and surrender which we know they neither mean for themselves nor have any intention of fulfilling for the child? Christian conscience can only reply to these questions with a downright "No!" One is thankful that this whole matter is receiving the careful attention and thought of many Church leaders today, but the custom remains widespread and disturbing.

Supposing we raised our standards and stopped our compromises? Supposing we proclaimed our message and tightened our discipline with love but without fear? I will tell you the result: the Church would suffer. There would be an outcry. We should be called puritanical, Victorian, old-fashioned, unpractical, rigid. Indeed, every imaginable derogatory epithet would be called into the service of the unbelieving world, and the Church would again find itself where it belongs—outside the gate, and in the wilderness.

I am not advocating a harsh lovelessness towards the weak, the sinful or the penitent. Nor am I recommending that we court opposition with rash and foolish indiscretion. I am simply suggesting that we should not compromise on clear, moral and spiritual issues. I am just saying that we should face this fact, namely, that if we do not suffer it is probably because we compromise and that if we do not compromise we certainly shall suffer.

Smyrna was a suffering church because it was an uncompromising church.

It is good to notice that the letter Christ addressed to Smyrna was not just a stern call to suffer and to endure. With the call to suffer there went a promise of accompanying grace. If Christ seldom makes offers without demands, He also seldom makes demands without offers. He offers His strength that we may meet His demands. So this epistle, so full of sufferings, is full of comforts and consolations also. Let us examine these now.

(2) THE COMFORTS THEY RECEIVED FROM CHRIST

Christ's words of command are clear. *Do not fear what you are about to suffer* and *Be faithful unto death* (v. 10). Here was an appeal to be faithful and not to be afraid. Now faith and fear are opposites. They cannot co-exist. Faith banishes fear. "When I am afraid", wrote the Psalmist (56: 3), "I put my trust in Thee". There is no other course to take. Jesus prescribed the same remedy. "Be not afraid" He used to say "only believe" (Mk. 5: 36). True, here the call is to faithfulness rather than to faith, but we need to remember that faith and faithfulness are the same word in Greek. This is understandable because it is from faith that faithfulness springs. Trust in Christ, and we shall ourselves be trustworthy. Rely on Christ, and we shall be reliable. Depend on Christ, and we shall be dependable. Have faith in Christ, and we shall be faithful—faithful if necessary even unto death. The way to lose fear is to gain faith.

But is Christ worthy of our trust when we suffer? It is just in time of tribulation that our faith falters. How then can our faith in Him grow so that whether in light or in darkness, in sunshine or in storm, we shall put our whole trust and confidence in Him? Well, He is worthy of our implicit faith because of who and what He is. It is this that the epistle discloses to the sufferer. Once let us grasp this revelation of Christ and our faith will be wonderfully strengthened and matured. He reveals here seven truths about himself.

(i) He is eternal. He is *the first and the last* (v. 8). He has already thus described Himself in the first chapter (v. 17), and attached to this declaration a command not to be afraid. His word to John was: "Fear not, I am the first and the last". In saying this He is only repeating in different words what the Lord God had said in chapter 1, verse 8: "I am the Alpha and the Omega". Jesus quietly assumes this divine title. He shares the eternal, immutable being of God. He is the beginning and the end. He is from everlasting to everlasting. In the midst of change He changes not. He "has neither beginning of days nor end of life" (Heb. 7: 3). He is "the same yesterday and today and for ever" (Heb. 13: 8). The seas of life may ebb and flow; He stands as immovable as a rock. We are born and grow and decay and die, but His years do not fail. Before we were born He was Alpha, and He will be Omega after we have passed from this earthly stage and are seen no more. When fears grip the heart of men, and name and goods and life are threatened, nothing can bring tranquillity like faith in Him who is both the first and the last and eternal.

(ii) He is victorious. He *died and came to life* (v. 8). Most men live and die; Christ died and lived! Does He appeal to us to *be faithful unto death*? It is because He Himself "became obedient unto death, even death on a cross" (Phil. 2: 8). Death, even violent death, should hold no terrors for us if we believe that Jesus not only experienced it but conquered it. He died. He remained dead. For about thirty-six hours He was held in the grip of death. But then He burst death's prison bars and emerged its triumphant victor. Now He is "the living one". He can say "I died, and behold I am alive for evermore". "The keys of Death and Hades" are in His hand (1: 18). He has roundly defeated him who had the power of death, that is the devil, so that He might free us from all fear of death (Heb. 2: 14, 15). The domain of death is under His sway.

(iii) He is all-knowing. He says *I know your tribulation* (v. 9). This is a great and sweet comfort. One of our greatest needs in trouble is someone with whom to share it. We long to unburden ourselves to somebody who understands. Now Jesus Christ is the world's greatest confidant. No friend or father confessor can bring to us the peace and the relief that He can bring. We can then sing with the old plantation negroes:

> Nobody knows the trouble I've seen;
> Nobody knows but Jesus.

He knows, however. He knows because He walks among the lampstands. His knowledge is not a distant acquaintance with facts; it is a close, personal understanding of people. His presence is never withdrawn. However deep our sorrow or great our suffering, He knows and cares.

(iv) He is balanced. That is, He has a right sense of proportion and a true perspective. He says: *I know . . . your poverty (but you are rich)*. His set of values is different from the world's. He looks not on our material, but on our spiritual, condition. Things are not in reality to Him what they often seem on the surface to us. We may be poor and at the same time rich. Those who lack much of this world's goods can yet be "rich toward God", "rich in faith", "rich in good deeds", and have "treasure in heaven" (Lk. 12: 21; Jas. 2: 5; 1 Tim. 6: 18; Mt. 6: 19, 20 and 19: 21). It is possible to be impoverished in material things and yet enriched in Christ in every way, enjoying "the unsearchable riches of Christ" (1 Cor. 1: 4; Eph. 3: 8). "Though He was rich, yet for your sake He became poor, so that by His poverty you might become rich" (2 Cor. 8: 9). The paradox is at its most dramatic when we can affirm with Paul that we are "as poor, yet making many rich; as having nothing, and yet possessing everything" (2 Cor. 6: 10).

How do we measure wealth? In terms of houses and cars, fur coats and television sets? Or in terms of God's priceless love, of a ripening character that will endure, of a faith more precious than gold and a wisdom more priceless than rubies, of spiritual treasure in heaven? Then enforced poverty will not alter our eternal riches, for in Archbishop Trench's words "there are both poor rich-men and rich poor-men in His sight". Let men despise us as poor, it matters not if Christ can add His reassuring parenthesis (*but thou art rich*). It is better to have it this way than to suffer from the blindness of the Laodicean church which said "I am rich" and to whom Christ had to say "you do not know that you are wretched, pitiable, poor, blind and naked" (3: 17). It is better too to hear this word of Christ about our wealth than to hear His description of the Jews. They *say that they are Jews and are not, but are a synagogue of Satan* (v. 9). They were not true Jews, because "he is not a real Jew who is one outwardly. . . . He is a Jew who is one inwardly. . . ." (Rom. 2: 28, 29). They say they are Jews, but they are not. They say you are poor, but you are not. In both their judgments they are mistaken. Then let us not be too greatly concerned by the opinions of the unbeliever. Let us rather cultivate the mind of Christ. It is His perspective which is true. Only He can see straight. All others are cross-eyed and squint.

(v) He is sovereign. He is in control. No suffering can engulf us but with His express permission. He has perfect knowledge of our present trials and perfect foreknowledge of our future tribulation. So He warns the Christians of Smyrna about what is to come, but He sets a limit to their sufferings. *Behold*, He says, *the devil is about to throw some of you into prison, . . . and for ten days you will have tribulation* (v. 10). You will see that only *some of you* will be imprisoned, and that the tribulation will last only *for ten days* (a short, unspecified but restricted period). So a limit is set both to the number of Christians who will have to suffer this ordeal and to its duration.

Christians who know that God is on the throne and is controlling the affairs of men can stand quiet and calm amid the evils and sorrows of the world. As with the pitiful afflictions of Job, and as with the mighty heathen empires which invaded Judah, God would say to the devil in Smyrna "thus far and no further".

(vi) He is purposeful. The devil's consignment of certain Christians of Smyrna to prison was *that you may be tested* (v. 10). This was Satan's self-confessed design. He was seeking to sift those believers as wheat is sifted when it is winnowed (cf. Lk. 22: 31). He desired the chaff to be blown away by the wind. But what Satan proposes, God permits. God too has a purpose in suffering, and although the details of His purpose are often obscure, His general intention is clear. Our adversary tempts in order to destroy; but our Father tests in order to refine. As gold is purified of dross in the furnace, so the fires of affliction can purge our Christian faith and strengthen our Christian character (Jas. 1: 2-4; 1 Pet. 1: 7). Let us then look beyond the trial to the purpose, beyond the pain of the chastening to its profit.

(vii) He is generous. He promises a rich reward to the Christian who is steadfast through suffering. *Be faithful unto death, and I will give you the crown of life. . . . He who conquers shall not be hurt by the second death* (vv. 10, 11). We have already seen that every letter ends with the promise of an appropriate reward. *I will give*, He says. It is not a merit award; it is a gift.

But Christ is generous in His gifts. If we endure, He says, and by our endurance prove the genuineness of our Christian profession, we shall escape the hell which is *the second death* (v. 11) and enter the heaven which is *the crown of life* (v. 10). We may need to be *faithful unto death*, but then *the second death* will not claim us. We may lose our life, but then *the crown of life* will be given us.

The crown of life (v. 10) is the same as *the tree of life* (v. 7), but the metaphor has changed. Heaven is now no longer a pleasure-garden and eternal life a tree bearing delicious fruit, but the winning-post at the end of a race and eternal life the victor's wreath or garland. Smyrna was famous for its arena and its games. So the Smyrna church will not have found it difficult to imagine the Christian life as a race or contest. It required diligent training, energy and strong exertion. The pace would be fast and the going hard. There would be sweat and pain. But at the end stood He who is the first and the last, the Victor *par excellence*, and in His hand was the crown of life which every conqueror would receive.

Here then is the message of the letter to the church of Smyrna which is as searching for us as it was for them: if we are true, we shall suffer. But let us be faithful and not fear. Jesus Christ, the first and the last, who died and lived again, knows our trials, controls our destiny, and will invest us with the crown of life at the end of the race.

4

THE LETTER TO PERGAMUM: TRUTH
(Rev. 2: 12-17)

*A ND to the angel of the church in Pergamum write: "The words
of him who has the sharp two-edged sword. I know where you
dwell, where Satan's throne is; you hold fast my name and you did
not deny my faith even in the days of Antipas my witness, my
faithful one, who was killed among you, where Satan dwells. But I
have a few things against you: you have some there who hold the
teaching of Balaam, who taught Balak to put a stumbling block before
the sons of Israel, that they might eat food sacrificed to idols and
practice immorality. So you also have some who hold the teaching of
the Nicolaitans. Repent then. If not, I will come to you soon and war
against them with the sword of my mouth. He who has an ear, let
him hear what the Spirit says to the churches. To him who conquers
I will give some of the hidden manna, and I will give him a white
stone, with a new name written on the stone which no one knows
except him who receives it".*

It is significant that Christ begins His letter to the church at
Pergamum by the statement *I know where you dwell* (v. 13). We
have already had occasion to observe that His knowledge of
the churches depends on His presence among them. He knows
them because He walks among them. In this letter, however,
He makes it clear that His intimate knowledge extends not only
to the works His people do (as in Ephesus) and to the tribulation
they endure (as in Smyrna) but to the environment in which

they live. *I know where you dwell*, He says. He is not ignorant of the fact that the Christian Church is set in the non-Christian world, and that it feels on all sides the continuous pressure of heathen influence. Christians are constantly aware that the pagan neighbours who surround them have different ideas, a different religion, a different philosophy. Their little boat is being tossed about by the winds and waves of strange doctrines. Their fortress is bombarded by the gunfire of alien cults. They feel besieged, beleaguered.

In no place was this more true than in Pergamum, which Professor Swete described as "a strong centre of paganism" (p. 33). Here a pitched battle was being fought, in which the soldiers were not men but ideas. Locked together in deadly combat, the issue was not between good and evil, but between truth and error.

Pergamum was about fifty-five miles from Smyrna, and as due north of it as Smyrna was of Ephesus. But it was some fifteen miles from the Aegean coast, and a mile or two from the River Caicus in whose valley it was situated. No traveller could visit Pergamum without being impressed by its welter of temples and altars. "The acropolis of Pergamum crowned a steep hill that rose one thousand feet above the plain. Near the summit stood an immense altar to Zeus, erected by Eumenes II to commemorate the victory won by his father over the Gauls; and at a short distance from this altar there was an elegant temple of Athena" (*Westminister Dictionary of the Bible*: "Pergamum"). Other deities honoured in Pergamum were Dionysos and particularly Asklepios or Aesculapius, the "Saviour God" or the god of healing, "the remains of whose magnificent temple outside the city *still remain*" (Trench p. 114). According to Tacitus and Xenophon, the worship of Aesculapius had its headquarters in Pergamum which thus became "the Lourdes of the Province of Asia, and the seat of a famous school of medicine" (R. H. Charles p. 60).

More important still was the well-developed cult of Rome

and Caesar which seems to have thrived in Pergamum. Back in 29 B.C. permission had been granted to the citizens of Pergamum to erect and dedicate a temple to Augustus. This was the first provincial temple to be built in honour of a living emperor. Smyrna's came three years later, in 26 B.C. "The imperial cult had thus its centre at Pergamum" (R. H. Charles p. 61).

It appears from this prevalence of religious superstition that antichrist was more evident in Pergamum than Christ. What had Christ to say to a church oppressed by such influence?

(1) CHRIST'S CONCERN FOR THE TRUTH

It is well to begin by observing that the exalted Christ is deeply concerned for the preservation and propagation of the truth. To this theme this whole letter is devoted. He commends the church because, He says, *you hold fast my name and you did not deny my faith* (v. 13), but He adds a complaint that although they had maintained their own theological conviction uncontaminated, they tolerated in their fellowship some false prophets. *But I have a few things against you: you have some there who hold the teaching of Balaam* (v. 14). Instead of "holding" Christ's name, they were "holding" a false cult (the Greek verb is the same), and this was deeply disturbing to the church's Heavenly Overseer. This guarding of the truth of the gospel unsullied and unspoiled is a real concern of Jesus Christ. He is not only anxious that we should love Him and that we should suffer bravely for Him, but also that we should believe in Him and hold the truth about Him.

It is specially striking that if in these letters love is the first mark of a true and living church, truth is the third, because the Scriptures hold love and truth together in perfect balance. Some Christians are so resolved to make love paramount, that they forget the sacredness of revealed truth. "Let us drown our doctrinal differences", they urge, "in the ocean of brotherly love!" Others are equally mistaken in their pursuit of truth at the expense of love. So dogged is their zeal for God's word that they become harsh and bitter and unloving. Love becomes sentimental if it is not strengthened by truth, and truth becomes hard if it is not softened by love. We need to preserve the balance of the Bible which tells us to hold the truth in love, to love others in the truth, and to grow not only in love but in discernment (Eph. 4: 15; 3 Jn. 1; Phil. 1: 9).

Let those who say that it does not matter what you believe so long as you live well and love all, read, mark, learn and inwardly digest this epistle. Let them consider the attitude and gain the mind of our Lord Jesus Christ. He does not share the lack of doctrinal concern exhibited by such. He called Himself "the truth" and "the light of the world". He promised His disciples that if they continued in His word they would know the truth and the truth would liberate them. He told Pontius Pilate that He had come into the world to bear witness to the truth (Jn. 14: 6; 8: 12, 31-32; 18: 37). He loves the truth, He speaks the truth, He is the truth. Then how can we be indifferent to it?

At Pergamum most church members were continuing to walk in the truth. Only a few, whether in full fellowship or in casual association with the church, had departed from the narrow path of revelation and wandered into the byways of speculation and error. But the risen Christ, the Chief Shepherd of His flock, was grieved both by the waywardness of the minority and by the nonchalance of the majority. *You have some there who hold the teaching of Balaam . . . you also have some who hold the teaching of the Nicolaitans* (vv. 14, 15), He complains. Do you not care that the robe of truth is being allowed to trail in the mud? Does it mean nothing to you that my name is being dishonoured by some and my faith denied? *Repent then!* (v. 16).

But what is truth, as (in Bacon's famous phrase) Pilate asked "and would not stay for an answer"? Was the situation in Pergamum really as serious as Christ appears to suggest? I hope to show in the next chapter that the epistles to Pergamum and Thyatira leave room for debate and disagreement on peripheral matters, while insisting that the central Christian truths cannot be compromised. How wise was Rupert Meldenius in the seventeeth century, whom Richard Baxter quotes in his *Reformed Pastor* as saying: "Sit in necessariis unitas, in non necessariis libertas, in omnibus caritas". We must learn to preserve unity in essentials, liberty in non-essentials and charity in all things. Many of our troubles in inter-church relations arise from our lack of proportion. We minimize the central and magnify the circumferential. We often make concessions on clearly revealed truths which should never be surrendered, and yet insist upon secondary matters or even on trivialities which are neither revealed nor required by God.

What then are these central truths? I believe they can be reduced to two, both of which are implicit in this epistle to Pergamum.

The first is a doctrinal truth concerning Christ. It has been rightly said that Christianity is Christ. Jesus Christ Himself is the rock on which the structure of Christian theology is built. To be a Christian is to accept Jesus Christ as God and Saviour. The irreducible minimum of Christian belief is that Jesus of Nazareth is the unique Son of God and that He died to be the Saviour of the world. I may not fully understand either statement (the Incarnation and the Atonement are two of the profoundest mysteries of the Christian creed), but if I want to call myself a Christian I must believe both. I must not only believe them intellectually; I must act on them. If my intellectual conviction is genuine, it will lead me to a personal commitment. If Jesus is *the* divine Lord, I must submit to Him as *my* Lord. If He is *the* divine Saviour, I must trust in Him as *my* Saviour. I must humbly appropriate the Son of God and Saviour of men as my Saviour and my Lord.

All this is implied in the two phrases by which the Lord Jesus describes the Christians of Pergamum. *You hold fast my name and you did not deny my faith* (v. 13). What does He mean by *my name* and *my faith*? His name stands for Himself. It is the revelation of who He is and what He has done. It represents the fulness of His divine person and saving work. To *hold fast* His name is therefore firmly to believe that He is the divine Lord and Saviour, thoughtfully to grip on to this conviction and never to let it go. The phrase *my faith* takes us a stage further. Commentators are agreed that, grammatically speaking, *my faith* means "your faith in me". We have already seen that it is not enough to assent intellectually to the fact of Christ's Lordship and Saviourhood; we must put our trust in Him personally as our own Saviour and Lord. We must not only hold fast His name but exercise faith in Him.

These fundamental truths cannot be compromised. The New Testament apostles make this abundantly clear. We cannot have Christian fellowship with those who deny the divinity of Christ's person or the satisfactoriness of His work on the cross for our salvation. These are defence positions we cannot yield. There is no room for negotiation or appeasement here. To deny that Jesus of Nazareth was both human and divine, "the Christ come in the flesh" is antichrist, wrote John, while to preach any other gospel than the gospel of Christ's saving grace is to deserve Paul's anathema (1 Jn. 2: 22; 4: 2, 3; 2 Jn. 7-11; Gal. 1: 6-9).

The Pergamene Christians' grasp of these central truths had evidently been put to a severe test. They had been sorely tempted to give in. But they had stood firm. They had not followed the cowardly example of Peter who denied Jesus. They had not denied Christ's faith; they had held fast His name. Indeed, one of their number in the heat of the persecution had been faithful even unto death. We know nothing of him except what may be gathered here. His name was Antipas. This was probably his real name, although I confess to a sneaking regret that most scholars have rejected the fanciful idea suggested by E. W. Hengstenberg in 1850 that like other names in the Revelation this too is symbolical. In defiance of grammar its Greek words would then be made to mean "against everyone", and Antipas would appear as an early *Athanasius contra mundum*, who dared to stand alone against all the enemies of Christ. His courage cost him his life, and Jesus accords to him His own title "faithful witness" (1: 5; 3: 14) when He refers to him affectionately as *Antipas my witness, my faithful one, who was killed among you* (v. 13).

It is not hard to reconstruct the scene which probably saw the death of Antipas. Known to be a Christian, he was summoned before the Proconsul of the Province, whose official residence is thought by some to have been in Pergamum. This civil leader was also chief priest of the imperial cult. A bust of the emperor was set on a plinth, and sacred fire burned before it. To sacrifice to the genius of Rome and the divine Emperor was a simple matter. All he had to do was to sprinkle a few grains of incense on the fire and say "Kurios Kaisar", "Caesar is Lord". Then he would be released. But how could he deny Christ's name and faith? Had he not at his baptism been proud to affirm his faith, in the simple words "Kurios Iesous", "Jesus is Lord"? Had he not been instructed that God had exalted Jesus to His own right hand and set Him far above all principality and power and every name that is named, and given Him the name that is above every name that at the name of Jesus every knee should bow, and that every tongue should confess that Jesus Christ is Lord to the glory of God the Father? Had his teachers not assured him that to say "Jesus is Lord" was a sign of the Holy Spirit's inspiration, whereas no man can say "Jesus be cursed" when speaking by the Spirit of God (Eph. 1: 20, 21; Phil. 2: 9-11; 1 Cor. 12: 3)? Such thoughts as these will have invaded the mind of Antipas as his Christian faith was exposed to its supreme test. Whether he wavered or not, we cannot say. All we know is that he was given grace to stand firm, to hold fast Christ's name and not to deny Christ's faith. He would indeed render to Caesar the things that were Caesar's, but he must also render to God the things that were God's. He could not bring himself to give to Caesar the title that belonged to Christ. Christ was his Lord, not Caesar, even if it meant the whip, the sword, the lions or the stake. So Antipas joined "the noble army of martyrs". He was a faithful witness, and sealed his testimony with his blood.

The second central Christian truth which cannot at any price be sacrificed is an ethical truth concerning holiness. The Christian faith in its fundamentals concerns the person and work of Christ on the one hand and the life of righteousness on the other. Christianity in essence exalts Christ and promotes holiness. To deny Christ and to follow sin are to surrender the citadel of Christianity to the enemy and to haul down the standard of truth. The New Testament writers insist dogmatically on the defence of these two bastions. They are as savage in their denunciation of immoral people as they are in their repudiation of those who forsake Christ and His gospel. Other lesser matters can be condoned, as has already been mentioned, but these never. There is room for a difference of opinion about minor points of doctrine and ethics, but here there must be absolute unanimity and no compromise. St. John's first epistle is devoted to this theme, that he who is born of God both believes in Christ and practises righteousness, walks in the truth and walks in the light. To deny that Jesus is the Christ is to be a liar; to claim to know God and to disobey His commandments is to be a liar also. Similarly, the apostle Paul urges the Corinthians not to associate with any Christian brother if by choice and practice "he is guilty of immorality or greed, or is an idolater, reviler, drunkard, or robber—not even to eat with such a one" (1 Jn. 2: 4, 22; 1 Cor. 5: 11).

This vehement rejection of sin and this passionate love of righteousness emerge clearly from the epistle to the church of Pergamum. The Pergamene Christians harboured in their midst some who held *the teaching of Balaam* and *the teaching of the Nicolaitans* (vv. 14, 15). It is commonly agreed that the Balaamites and the Nicolaitans were the same teachers, and are not to be distinguished from each other. They were to be found in the church of Ephesus. Why they were called *Nicolaitans* we have discussed in connection with the letter to that church. We must now enquire what was their relation to Balaam.

It will be remembered that Balaam was a remarkable prophet whose story is told in chapters 22 to 24 of the Book of Numbers. Balak, the King of Moab, summoned him to come and curse the tribes of Israel who were about to cross over the River Jordan into the Promised Land. But every time Balaam opened his mouth, the words the Lord gave him to speak were words not of cursing but of blessing. Moved (according to 2 Pet. 2: 15 and Jude 11) by greed for the reward Balak was offering him, Balaam devised another scheme for the downfall of Israel. He suggested to Balak that Moabite girls should seduce the Israelite men, by inviting them to take part in their idolatrous and immoral feasts. He knew, and knew rightly, that this would provoke the righteous God of Israel to anger. So *Balaam . . . taught Balak to put a stumbling block before the sons of Israel, that they might eat food sacrificed to idols and practise immorality* (v. 14; cf. Num. 25 and 31: 16).

What Balaam was to the old Israel the Nicolaitans were to the new. They were insinuating their vile doctrines into the camp of the Israel of God. They dared to suggest that the liberty with which Christ has made us free was a liberty to sin. "Christ has redeemed us from the law", they argued. "Therefore we are no longer under law but under grace. And so", their specious villainy continued, "we may continue in sin that God's grace may continue to abound towards us in forgiveness." This terrible travesty of the truth was to "pervert the grace of our God into licentiousness and deny our only Master and Lord, Jesus Christ" (Gal. 5: 1; Rom. 6: 1; Jude 4).

"Just a little idolatry", they murmured. "Just a little immorality. We are free. We do not have to go to extremes." Such blatant reasoning is sometimes heard in the churches today. "A man must have his fling", it is said. "It is no use being idealistic. We are all human, you know. Christ does not expect too much from us. His demands are not unreasonable. He knows we are dust." Totally different is Christ's view of this matter. Some manuscripts conclude verse 15 (as in the Authorized Version): . . . *the teaching of the Nicolaitans, which thing I hate*. The words may not be original here, but they are true. Sin to Christ is "that abominable thing which I hate". The church of Ephesus hated "the works of the Nicolaitans" (v. 6), and were commended for their holy hatred. Christ even adds in that epistle "I also hate" them. But what was hated in Ephesus was tolerated in Pergamum. So Christ calls the church to *repent* (v. 16), to repent of its error and its evil, for He is deeply concerned about a church which is tainted with such things.

(2) CHRIST'S RECOGNITION OF THE SOURCE OF ERROR

We turn from a consideration of Christ's concern for the truth to note His recognition of the origin of error. It is diabolical. The church of Pergamum lived and worshipped and witnessed *where Satan dwells* (v. 13b), *where Satan's throne is* (v. 13a). Satan not only inhabited Pergamum, but ruled it. Pergamum was not only his home, but his throne. The implication is clear in the context, that Satan is the source of the errors to which the church was there exposed.

Let us rid our minds of the medieval caricature of Satan. Forget the horns, the hooves and the tail, and we are left with the Biblical portrait of a spiritual being, highly intelligent, immensely powerful and utterly unscrupulous. A recent Gallup poll arranged by the *News Chronicle*, to enquire into the religious beliefs and practices of the British people, revealed the interesting fact that only 24 per cent of people under twenty-one believed in the devil. How delighted he must be! But no Christian can so easily dispatch this unclean spirit in whose existence our Lord certainly believed. Christ not only accepted his existence, but taught about his power. He called him "the ruler of this world", much as St. Paul called him "the prince of the power of the air". He has therefore a throne and a kingdom, and under him there swarms an array of malignant spirits who are described in Scripture as "principalities and powers", "the world rulers of this present darkness" and "the spiritual hosts of wickedness in the heavenly places" (Jn. 12: 31; Eph. 2: 2; 6: 12).

But Satan and his army have been overthrown. Christ saw Satan fall like lightning from heaven, and John later in the Revelation describes how the dragon and his angels were defeated by Michael and his angels and "thrown down". At the cross Jesus met and conquered all the forces of evil. As they closed in upon Him, He stripped them off from Him like a filthy garment, and "made a public example of them, triumphing over them". There Satan's head was crushed, although in the doing of it Christ's heel was bruised (Lk. 10: 18; Rev. 12:7-12; Col. 2: 15; Gen. 3: 15).

Despite their overthrow, the powers of darkness continue to contest every inch of their territory. The kingdom of Satan retreats only as the kingdom of God advances. In some places he holds almost undisputed sway. Pergamum was such a place. *I know where you dwell*, says Jesus to the church, *you dwell . . . where Satan dwells* (v. 13). Its multitudinous temples, shrines and altars, its labyrinth of antichristian philosophies, its grant of refuge to antinomian Nicolaitans and Balaamites, all bore eloquent testimony to the dominion of the evil one. Perhaps in mentioning Satan, who is "that ancient serpent" (12: 9), Christ is making a veiled allusion to the cult of Aesculapius, whose symbol was a serpent. Perhaps also *Satan's throne* refers to the massive altar to Zeus Soter "which seemed to dominate the place from its platform cut in the Acropolis rock" (Swete). But the chief menace of Satan lay in the claims of the imperial religion. It was through a refusal to take part in this that Antipas had lost his life. It was here that the dragon's authority was most clearly seen.

So Pergamum was a dark place. The light of truth filtered but weakly into it. It was steeped in the dense fogs of error. For Satan is "the power of darkness" and is the ruler of "this present darkness" and "hates the light" (Lk. 22: 53; Eph. 6: 12; Jn. 3: 20). He is called in Scripture both a liar and a deceiver. He is said to blind the minds of the unbelievers. He not only entices mortals into sin but beguiles them into error (Jn. 8: 44; 2 Cor. 4: 4). Later in this book we are introduced to the dragon's allies, and one of them is "the beast which rose out of the earth" who is later called "the false prophet", whose function is to make "the earth and its inhabitants worship the first beast" (13: 11, 12; 19: 20). If the first beast which rose out of the sea and whom men worshipped stands for the persecuting Roman Empire, the second no doubt represents the emperor-cult.

The emperor-cult has long since vanished, but with it "the false prophet" has not died. He lives again in every non-Christian religion and philosophy, and in every attempt to divert to others the honour that is due to Jesus Christ alone. This is the spirit of antichrist. This is the work of Satan.

(3) CHRIST'S RESOLVE THAT TRUTH SHALL TRIUMPH OVER ERROR

Concerned that His church shall stand in the truth, and recognizing the source of error, Jesus Christ is resolved that the truth shall triumph. He calls upon the church which has permitted grievous error to be taught unchecked to *repent* (v. 16), and to gain the victory over falsehood. He then indicates both the way of conquest and its reward.

The way of conquest is by His word. The only weapon which can slay the forces of error is Christ's word. No wonder, as Christ dictates this epistle to John, He designates Himself He *who has the sharp two-edged sword* (v. 12). In the vision of the exalted Christ which John saw and described in the first chapter of the Revelation, this sharp two-edged sword issued from His mouth (1: 16), because it is a symbol of the word of truth which proceeds from Christ's lips. Indeed, He is Himself "The word of God" (Rev. 19: 13, cf. Jn. 1: 1). The picture of Christ with a sword flashing from His mouth may seem to us most peculiar, but it is "not so strange as appears at first sight, for the short Roman sword was tongue-like in shape" (Hastings' *Dictionary of the Bible* iv. p..634, quoted by Swete p. 18). Already in the prophecy of Isaiah the Servant of the Lord, prefiguring Christ, says of the Lord: "He made my mouth like a sharp sword" (49: 2). The word of God is said by St. Paul to be "the sword of the Spirit" and in the Epistle to the Hebrews to be "living and active, sharper than any two-edged sword, piercing to the division of soul and spirit, of joints and marrow, and discerning the thoughts and intentions of the heart" (Eph. 6: 17; Heb. 4: 12). Whether or not we agree with Tertullian and Augustine that the two edges of the sword represent the Old and New Testaments, the Bible has many sword-like qualities. It pricks the conscience, and wounds the pride, of sinners. It cuts away our camouflage and pierces our defences. It lays bare our sin and need, and kills all false doctrine by its deft, sharp thrusts.

God's way to overcome error is the proclamation of the gospel of Christ which is God's power of salvation to everyone who believes. Falsehood will not be suppressed by the gruesome methods of the inquisition, or by the burning of heretics at the stake, or by restrictive State legislation, or even by war. Force of arms cannot conquer ideas. Only truth can defeat error. The false ideologies of the world can be overthrown only by the superior ideology of Christ. We have no other weapons but this sword. Let us use it fearlessly, and by the open manifestation of the truth storm the strongholds of Satan.

> O God of truth, whose living word
> Upholds whate'er hath breath,
> Look down on Thy creation, Lord,
> Enslaved by sin and death.

> Set up Thy standard, Lord, that we
> Who claim a heavenly birth

    May march with Thee to smite the lies
    That vex Thy ransomed earth.

One day this same sword will change its function. The
message of truth will become the message of judgment. The
sword to pierce the conscience will be the sword to destroy
the soul. *I will come to you soon and war against them with the
sword of my mouth* (v. 16). Again, "from His mouth issues a
sharp sword with which to smite the nations, and He will rule
them with a rod of iron . . . and the rest were slain by . . . the
sword that issues from His mouth" (19: 15, 21). Balaam himself
was killed with the sword (Num. 31: 8; Josh. 13: 22), and the
Balaamites in Pergamum would suffer the same fate, unless
they repented. The sword of Christ's word would devour them.
This being interpreted means that the very gospel of Christ
which saves those who obey it destroys those who disobey it.
If anything is certain about divine judgment in Scripture, it is
that God will hold us responsible for our reaction to that measure
of truth which we have heard. And to whom much is revealed,
from him much will be required. Did not Jesus say to His
contemporaries: "If any one hears my sayings and does not
keep them, I do not judge him . . . he who rejects me and does
not receive my sayings has a judge; the word that I have spoken
will be his judge on the last day" (Jn. 12: 47, 48). Here is Christ's
saving word turned judge, Christ's wholesome sword turned
executioner. Let us ourselves beware, and submit to this word
before it condemn us.

Having outlined God's weapon for the conquest of error,
Christ now describes His reward to the conqueror. That is to
the man or woman who hears and receives His word, seeks to
understand it and strives to live by it. *To him who conquers I will
give some of the hidden manna, and I will give him a white stone,
with a new name written on the stone which no one knows except him
who receives it* (v. 17).

Here are two precious and desirable gifts, the hidden manna

and a white stone inscribed with a new name. What do these presents mean? The hiddenness of the manna no doubt alludes to the "golden urn holding the manna" which was kept in the ark (Ex. 16: 32-34; Heb. 9: 4), but the manna itself is Christ. Just as the old Israel were fed by manna in the wilderness, so the new Israel have their soul's hunger satisfied by Christ, the bread of life. He Himself, after feeding the five thousand, claimed to be "the true bread from heaven . . . which . . . gives life to the world" (Jn. 6: 31-35) and "the living bread which came down from heaven" so that "if any one eats of this bread, he will live for ever" (Jn. 6: 48-51). But the promised reward with which each of the seven letters closes is a reward to be inherited in heaven, not on earth. So it is that our souls which already on earth taste Christ, our spiritual manna, will feast upon Him for ever in heaven. Denying ourselves the luxury of idol-meats in this life, the banquet will be the richer in the next.

As for the white stone inscribed with the new name, commentators have tumbled over one another with the rich variety of their interpretations. Some refer us to the jewels which, according to Rabbinical tradition, fell from the sky with the manna. Others write of the white ballot pebble thrown into a box by the judge when he acquitted a prisoner, while yet others remind us of the "tessara" given to winners in the games, entitling them to free access to the public entertainments. Stones were used as amulets, as counters and as tickets, and all these have been suggested for consideration here. But to me Archbishop Trench's explanation is the most reasonable. He recalls how the mysterious "Urim and Thummim", mentioned many times in the Old Testament, were consulted by the High Priest when he sought to receive divine guidance. They were connected with the twelve precious stones, symbolizing the twelve tribes of Israel, which were set in the High Priest's breastplate. The Urim, Trench thought, may have been a "white stone" or diamond on which was written, it has often been conjectured, the secret name of God. Since the pot of manna was hidden within the veil (which was entered only by the High Priest) and since the Urim was possessed and consulted by the High Priest only, Trench suggested that the manna and stone to be presented to the Christian conqueror are "both representing high priestly prerogatives which the Lord should at length impart to all His people, kings and priests to God" (p. 134).

Whatever the stone may be, the new name to be engraved on it is undoubtedly the name of Christ who says later in His letter to the Philadelphian church: "I will write on him . . . my own new name" (3: 12). The name is secret, just as the manna is hidden, for it will be disclosed only to him who receives it. What will be written on the white stone will be *a new name . . . which no one knows except him who receives it* (v. 17). The intimate self-revelation promised by Christ to the believer in paradise will be private and personal. Heaven will indeed be a community, but that does not mean that we shall be like a herd of indistinguishable cattle. We shall retain our individuality and our personal relationship to Christ.

> "Write Thy new name upon my heart
> Thy new, best name of love".

What then is the promise of the manna and the name on the stone? It is the pledge of a fuller revelation to him who holds fast the revelation already granted. The hidden manna is Christ. The new name is Christ. We shall feast on the manna and comprehend the name. This is the beatific vision. It will be to receive such a manifestation of Christ as shall completely satisfy both heart and mind. He who holds fast Christ's name shall receive a deeper revelation of it, *a new name*. He who does not deny Christ's faith shall be satisfied by the hidden manna. He who knows in part shall know as also he is known. He who sees Christ now in a mirror dimly shall see Him face to face. He who knows Christ now by faith shall afterwards receive "the fruition of His glorious Godhead".

So, recognizing Christ's concern for the triumph of His truth and Satan's activity in the spread of lies, let us guard what has been entrusted to us and "contend for the faith which was once for all delivered to the saints" (1 Tim. 6: 20; Jude 3), and hold the truth in love.

> *"I have this against you, that you tolerate the woman Jezebel"* Rev. 2: 20

5

THE LETTER TO THYATIRA: HOLINESS
(Rev. 2: 18-29)

*A*ND *to the angel of the church in Thyatira write: "The words of the Son of God, who has eyes like a flame of fire, and whose feet are like burnished bronze. I know your works, your love and faith and service and patient endurance, and that your latter works exceed the first. But I have this against you, that you tolerate the woman Jezebel, who calls herself a prophetess and is teaching and beguiling my servants to practise immorality and to eat food sacrificed to idols. I gave her time to repent, but she refuses to repent of her immorality. Behold, I will throw her on a sickbed, and those who commit adultery with her I will throw into great tribulation, unless they repent of her doings; and I will strike her children dead. And all the churches shall know that I am he who searches mind and heart, and I will give to each of you as your works deserve. But to the rest of you in Thyatira, who do not hold this teaching, who have not learned what some call the deep things of Satan, to you I say, I do not lay upon you any other burden; only hold fast what you have, until I come. He who conquers and who keeps my works until the end, I will give him power over the nations, and he shall rule them with a rod of iron, as when earthen pots are broken in pieces, even as I myself have received power from my Father; and I will give him the morning star. He who has an ear, let him hear what the Spirit says to the churches."*

"The longest letter is addressed to the least important of the Seven Cities". So Archdeacon R. H. Charles begins his commentary on this epistle (p. 67). The city of Thyatira was certainly smaller and less significant than the previous three. It was situated about half-way between Pergamum and Sardis on the great circular road of the Province of Asia to which reference has already been made. The postman entrusted with the delivery of these letters, having begun his round at Ephesus and travelled due north to Smyrna and farther north to Pergamum, will have had then to turn south-east and journey forty miles in order to reach Thyatira.

If Thyatira was noted for anything, it had a commercial rather than a political distinction. It was evidently at that time a prosperous trading centre. Inscriptions which archaeologists have brought to light reveal the interesting fact that Thyatira boasted numerous trade guilds. There were, for example, associations for bakers and bronze-workers, for clothiers and cobblers, for weavers, tanners, dyers and potters. It was from Thyatira that Lydia, one of Philippi's most notable converts, had come. She traded in materials treated with Thyatira's purple dye and is described by Luke as "a seller of purple goods" (Acts 16: 14). She had emigrated (perhaps on business) to Philippi in Macedonia, of which Thyatira was a colony, and there she heard Paul preach the gospel. The Lord opened her heart to listen to the message. She believed and was baptized.

Perhaps it was Lydia, newborn in Christ, who returned to her home in Thyatira and was the means of planting the Christian Church there. We do not know. Certainly by the time the Revelation was written, this prosperous city had a prosperous church. Jesus Christ speaks of it in words of warmest commendation. *I know your works*, He writes, *your love and faith and service and patient endurance* (v. 19). Here are four sterling Christian qualities indeed. Thyatira had not only rivalled Ephesus in busy Christian service, but also had the love which Ephesus lacked; preserved the faith which was imperilled at Pergamum; and shared with Smyrna the virtue of patient endurance in tribulation. Indeed, Thyatira's church was like a beautiful garden in which the fairest Christian graces blossomed; both a humble ministry on the one hand, and on the other that trinity so often described by St. Paul: faith, hope and charity. Faith and love are mentioned by name, and what is "patient endurance" but the fruit of hope? One is reminded forcibly of Paul's description of the Thessalonian believers' "work of faith and labour of love and steadfastness of hope in our Lord Jesus Christ" (1 Thess. 1: 3). Here too at Thyatira was a practical love resulting in service, and a virile faith and hope tending to endurance.

Nor is Thyatira's catalogue of virtues exhausted yet. *I know your works*, says Christ, and adds: *and that your latter works exceed the first* (v. 19). Thyatira had learned the oft-forgotten lesson that the Christian life is a life of growth, of progress, of development. Ephesus was backsliding; Thyatira was moving forward. The church of Ephesus had abandoned the love it had at first; the church of Thyatira was exceeding the works it did at first. Which of these two churches do we resemble more? Alas! that of many Christians the solemn words could be used: "the last state has become worse for them than the first" (2 Pet. 2: 20; cf. Mt. 12: 45). Very different is the ideal that is set before us in the New Testament. There the Christian life is variously illustrated. Now it is like the gradual maturing of a human being, from infancy through adolescence to adult stature; now it is the increasing fruitfulness of a vine; and now the chemical process employed for the refinement of metals. All these similes imply a movement which is steady but sure, positive and purposive. Is our Christian life like that? We began well, no doubt. But how are we faring now? Are we standing still, or falling back, or going on? The New Testament speaks of a growth in faith and love, in knowledge and holiness. St. Paul could rejoice, when writing a second letter to the Thessalonians, "because your faith is growing abundantly, and the love of every one of you for one another is increasing" (2 Thess. 1: 3). The Christians of Thyatira also were growing— growing in *love and faith and service and patient endurance* (v. 19).

In view of this splendid record, it is tragic to read a little further and discover this church's moral compromise. In that fair field a poisonous weed was being allowed to luxuriate. In that healthy body a malignant cancer had begun to form. An enemy was being harboured in the midst of the fellowship. *But I have this against you*, the letter continues, *that you tolerate the woman Jezebel, who calls herself a prophetess and is teaching and beguiling my servants to practise immorality and to eat food sacrificed to idols* (v. 20). The church of Thyatira manifested love and faith, service and endurance, but holiness is not included among its qualities. Indeed, it is this which was missing. It permitted one of its members to teach outrageous licence and apparently made no attempt to restrain her. In this too the church of Thyatira was the opposite of the church of Ephesus. Ephesus could not bear evil, self-styled apostles but had no love (2: 2, 4); Thyatira had love but tolerated an evil, self-styled prophetess.

Holiness of life, righteousness of character, is then another indispensable mark of the real Christian and of the true church. "This is the will of God, your sanctification: that you abstain from immorality". It is the purpose of the Father's election: "He chose us in Him (*sc.* Christ) before the foundation of the world, that we should be holy and blameless before Him". It is the purpose of the Son's death: "Jesus Christ . . . gave Himself for us to redeem us from all iniquity and to purify for Himself a people of His own who are zealous for good deeds". It is the purpose of the Holy Spirit's indwelling: "God has not called us for uncleanness, but in holiness . . . who gives His Holy Spirit to you" (1 Thess. 4: 3; Eph. 1: 4; Tit. 2: 13, 14; 1 Thess. 4: 7, 8). Here then are the Father, the Son and the Holy Spirit, the three glorious Persons of the one eternal Godhead, united in Their purpose to make us holy. But if it is God's purpose to make us holy, Satan is resolved to frustrate it. He is seeking ceaselessly both to entice individual Christian believers into sin, and to insinuate evil into the churches. Where he cannot muzzle the church's witness by persecution from without, he resorts to the subtler assault of pollution from within. If the dragon's two beasts fail, there is still the harlot Babylon with her loathsome charms. If the beast from the sea cannot crush the church by force, nor the beast from the earth silence the testimony of Christians by the errors of his false cult, then the Babylonian harlot's finery and jewels and pearls may seduce them and her golden cup poison them with its impure abominations (cf. 17: 1-6). Or, to drop the vivid imagery of the Revelation, if the devil cannot conquer the church by the application of political pressure or the propagation of intellectual heresy, he will try the insinuation of moral evil. Such at least was the dragon's foul strategy in Thyatira.

But who was *that woman Jezebel*? There is no need to go to the extremes of supposing either that there was a real woman of that name in Thyatira or that the expression merely represents an evil influence. She was a real woman all right, but the name is surely as symbolical as other Old Testament names in this book like Balaam, Sodom, Babylon and Jerusalem? What is meant is that this disreputable prophetess was as wicked and dangerous an influence in Thyatira as Jezebel had been in Israel.

Let me remind you of the history of that disgraceful woman, Queen Jezebel. She was the wife of Ahab, himself one of the weakest kings of Israel. She was a foreigner, who had imported into Israel an alien cult. Her father, Ethbaal by name, was a priest of Astarte who had succeeded to the throne of Sidon by murdering his predecessor. Astarte, or Ashtaroth, was the Phoenician equivalent of the Greek Aphrodite and the Roman Venus. Her beastly system had engineered such a complete divorce of morality from religion that it even encouraged gross sexual immorality under the cloak of piety. According to one etymology "Jezebel" (like our English "Agnes") means "pure" or "chaste"; but Jezebel contradicted her name by her character and her behaviour. When she married King Ahab, she became active in the diffusion of her revolting doctrines in Israel. She may even have been a priestess of Astarte herself. She persuaded the king to build a temple and altar to Astarte in his capital, Samaria. She supported eight hundred and fifty prophets of her immoral cult and killed off all the prophets of righteous Jehovah on whom she could lay her hands. She became well-known for what Jehu later called her "harlotries and sorceries" (1 Kings 16: 30-32; 18: 4, 19; 21: 25, 26; 2 Kings 9: 22). She sought to contaminate Israel, as Balaam had done before her, and Ahab did not possess the moral conviction or stamina to withstand her.

This first Jezebel had been dead nearly a thousand years. She met a horrible end. But her evil spirit had, as it were, become reincarnate in a prophetess of the first century A.D. Her religion too had little connection with morality. Laying claim to divine inspiration, she was succeeding in beguiling the servants of Christ to indulge in immoral practices. R. H. Charles thought that she was encouraging the Christians of Thyatira to attend the ceremonies and feasts of the local trade-guilds which were "dedicated no doubt to some pagan deity" and "too often ended in unbridled licentiousness" (pp. 69-70). This new Jezebel and her followers prided themselves on their mature experience of life. Like the later Gnostics, they were delving into the secret mysteries of which they boasted a private, esoteric revelation denied to the mass of Christians. They were a spiritual aristocracy, a favoured élite. The rank and file could not compete with them. They bragged that they plumbed "the deep things". Perhaps they even borrowed this phrase from St. Paul who spoke several times in his epistles of "the deep things of God"—the deeps of His wisdom and love which man cannot know but which the Holy Spirit searches out and explores (Rom. 11: 33; Eph. 3: 18; 1 Cor. 2: 10). The Gnostics borrowed the phrase but perverted it. With their diabolical theory that since matter was evil the sins of the flesh could be indulged without damage to the spirit, they plunged without restraint into what they called the *deep things* (v. 24)—deep things (as Christ ironically adds) *of Satan*, not of God.

The Jezebelites were then similar to, if not identical with, the

Nicolaitans and the Balaamites. Their practice of *immorality* and their eating of *food sacrificed to idols* (v. 20) are both mentioned in this epistle to Thyatira as in the earlier epistle to Pergamum (v. 14). Here, however, the emphasis seems to be on their sin rather than on their error, on a question of ethics rather than of doctrine. The church was allowing Jezebel and her brood to continue unchecked! Ephesus "hated" the works of the Nicolaitans and could not endure them (vv. 2, 6); Pergamum "had" some who held the doctrine of Balaam and of the Nicolaitans (vv.14, 15); but Thyatira actually "tolerated" them (v. 20). The Christians of Thyatira seem to have had either a very poor conscience or a very feeble courage. They were as weak and spineless towards the new Jezebel as Ahab had been towards the old. Christ complained that she had contrived to deceive His servants into sin. It is as if He said: "*My servants* (v. 20) are committed to obey me not Jezebel. To serve her is the licence which is slavery; to follow me is the service which is perfect freedom".

What message has the ascended Christ to a church in this condition?

(1) CHRIST'S STATEMENT TO THE WHOLE CHURCH

He begins His message to the Thyatira church as He begins the other letters, by saying: *I know*, but somehow in this letter the words have a more forceful meaning. All the churches needed to understand that He was their Heavenly Supervisor, walking among the lampstands, but Thyatira needed this assurance more than the rest, because many of the vile practices of the Jezebel party were being indulged in secret. Perhaps the church itself did not fully know what was going on behind locked doors and in the darkness. But Christ knew. He had good reason to introduce Himself to this church as *the Son of God, who has eyes like a flame of fire* (v. 18; cf. 1: 14; 19: 12). His burning eyes pierced the night which shrouded Jezebel's sins, and flashed with fiery indignation. The eyes of Jesus must have fascinated men when He was on earth. The Pharisees seemed to shrivel up in shame when "He looked around at them with anger, grieved at their hardness of heart", and Simon Peter could never erase from his imagination the gaze of those tender, loving, disappointed eyes as He "turned and looked at" him in the high priest's palace just after the cock crew (Mk. 3: 5; Lk. 22: 60, 61).

In this same letter Jesus calls Himself *He who searches mind and heart* (v. 23). This intimate knowledge of men's secret thoughts and motives is a divine faculty, frequently mentioned in the Old Testament, which *the Son of God* (v. 18) consciously claims to possess. Jeremiah, the prophet to whom was revealed perhaps more clearly than others the inwardness of religion and the importance of the heart, records God's word which Christ here quotes: "I the LORD search the mind and try the heart, to give to every man according to his ways. . . ." To this divine claim Jeremiah alludes when he prays: "O LORD of hosts, who judgest righteously, who triest the heart and the mind. . . ." So in the Acts of the Apostles God is twice given a name which in the Greek is a single noun and means "Heartknower" (Jer. 17: 10; 11: 20; cf. 20: 12 and Ps. 7: 9; Acts 1: 24; 15: 8).

The earthly Jesus had this ability too. He read men's thoughts and understood their hearts. Both His enemies and His disciples were amazed at His penetrating insight into the hidden places of their minds. Again and again we read of Him "perceiving in His spirit that they thus questioned within themselves", so that His closest followers reached the conclusion that nothing could be concealed from Him. "You know everything" was Peter's conviction, while John elaborated it a bit in his words: "He knew all men and needed no one to bear witness of man; for He Himself knew what was in man" (Mk. 2: 8; Jn. 21: 17; 2: 25). If this clearsighted scrutiny of the hearts and minds of men was a characteristic of the earthly Jesus, how much more must the risen Christ know all the secrets of men?

The wicked persuade themselves that their wickedness is not

known and will never come to light. "He does not see", they love to say about God, and "He will not judge". But it cannot be stated too emphatically both that God does see and that God will judge. "Woe to those who hide deep from the LORD their counsel, whose deeds are in the dark, and who say, 'Who sees us? Who knows?'" "Before Him no creature is hidden, but all are open and laid bare to the eyes of Him with whom we have to do", and "God judges the secrets of men by Christ Jesus" (Is. 29: 15; Heb. 4: 13; Rom. 2: 16). Let us then learn to live in the presence of Christ *who has eyes like a flame of fire* and who *searches mind and heart* (vv. 18, 23). His eyes run to and fro throughout the whole earth. He sees our downsitting and our uprising, and discerns our thoughts from afar. We cannot escape from His presence. His all-seeing eye is ever upon us. To remember this is a most powerful stimulus to holy living. It is what the Bible means by living "in the fear of the Lord".

(2) CHRIST'S WARNING TO THE JEZEBEL PARTY

Christ calls on this infamous group in Thyatira to repent. Indeed, they have already had an opportunity to do so, but have not yet availed themselves of it. *I gave her time to repent: but she refuses to repent of her immorality* (v. 21). Perhaps some warning had already been sent to Thyatira. We do not know what chance the Jezebel party had already been given. But we do know that God "is forbearing . . . , not wishing that any should perish, but that all should reach repentance". He has "no pleasure in the death of anyone"; He "desires all men to be saved" (2 Pet. 3: 9; Ezek. 18: 32; 1 Tim. 2: 4). That is His wish; but it was not Jezebel's. She "does not wish to repent", as the Greek phrase of verse 21 must be literally translated. Jesus Christ does not compel us to surrender, nor forcibly break the stubbornness of our will. He still says to us as He did years ago to impenitent Jerusalem: "How often would I have gathered your children together as a hen gathers her brood under her wings, and you would not!" (Mt. 23: 37). If Jezebel would not repent, however, there is still a glimmer of hope for her followers: *Those who commit adultery with her* will surely be punished, *unless they repent of their doings* (v. 22). The door of repentance was still open. There was still time. But the opportunity would not last for ever. One day, probably soon, it would pass.

If this final warning was not heeded, judgment would follow. *All the churches shall know that I am He who searches mind and heart, and I will give to each of you as your works deserve* (v. 23). He whose eyes flash like fire also has *feet . . . like burnished bronze* (v .18). The eyes that see into the hidden depths of our hearts can also blaze with righteous indignation, and His feet can trample us to powder. The nature of the coming judgment of the Jezebel party is couched in highly dramatic and partly symbolical terms, but let not the imagery of it blind us to its reality. *Behold I will throw her* (*sc.* Jezebel) *on a sickbed, and those who commit adultery with her I will throw into great tribulation . . . and I will strike her children dead* (vv. 22, 23). Her punishment will fit her crime. The scene of her wickedness will be the scene of her judgment. Her bed of sin will become a bed of sickness. The pleasures of sin will give place to the pains of tribulation, and her "spiritual progeny" (Swete p. 43), too deeply dyed with her evil to be cleansed, will be killed. Like the sons of Ahab and Jezebel, they too are doomed. That such literal physical punishments of sickness and death may have overtaken the immoral Jezebelites is most likely. This was the age in which Ananias and Sapphira fell dead because of their lying hypocrisy, and in which some Corinthian Christians had fallen ill and others had died because they had defiled the Lord's supper by their greed and irreverence (Acts 5: 1-11; 1 Cor. 11: 17-32). Let us be warned! We may not ourselves suffer an immediate physical judgment, but Christ's eyes are still as a flame of fire and His feet as strong as burnished brass, and "the unrighteous will not inherit the kingdom of God" (1 Cor. 6: 9).

(3) CHRIST'S ADVICE TO THE REST

Not all members of the church in Thyatira had been infected with the virus of Jezebel. Some had resisted her contagion. They did *not hold this teaching*. They had *not learned . . . the deep things of Satan* (v. 24). There was yet a godly remnant in Thyatira who had not defiled themselves. For these, whom Christ designates *the rest of you in Thyatira* (v. 24), He has a special word of advice. He says first *I do not lay upon you any other burden*, and then adds: *only hold fast what you have, until I come.* (vv. 24, 25). In the context, there is an unmistakable reference to the apostolic decree promulgated after the Jerusalem Conference described by Luke in Acts 15. This conference, which was presided over by James and in which Peter and Paul played a prominent part, reached the conclusion that a convert from heathenism did not have to be circumcised. That is, a Gentile did not need to become a Jew in order to be a Christian. But this exemption from the rite of circumcision did not signify freedom from the law of Moses. The decree therefore ended: "It has seemed good to the Holy Spirit and to us to lay upon you no greater burden than these necessary things: that you abstain from what has been sacrificed to idols and from blood and from what is strangled and from unchastity. If you keep yourselves from these, you will do well. Farewell" (Acts 15: 28, 29). Perhaps the two ceremonial prohibitions here ("blood" and "things strangled"), made in the early days of transition, are deliberately not re-enacted by Christ in His letter to Thyatira. The other two ("things sacrificed to idols" and "immorality") concerned the very two evils which had so grievously contaminated Thyatira. These two commands were still in force. If the church of Thyatira had remembered and obeyed the early apostolic decree, Christ's letter to them would not have been necessary. He does not lay on them *any other burden:* but urges them to *hold fast* what they have.

An important lesson lurks in these phrases, which we shall

do well to learn. It is this. A new immorality must not drive us into a new asceticism. We may be surrounded by unchastity, but we are not to let an extreme of laxity around us stampede us to an extreme of rigidity in ourselves. Christ has no new burden for those living in an environment where standards are low. We are simply to hold fast what we already have, that is to say, what He has already given us in His written word. What is this? It is the balanced, joyful, exhilarating righteousness of the Bible, the glorious liberty of the royal law. It is the sane morality which regards the right use of sex as beautiful and sacred, and its wrong use as ugly and sordid. It is the teaching which says: "Let marriage be held in honour among all, and let the marriage bed be undefiled; for God will judge the immoral and adulterous" (Heb. 13: 4).

God's commandments are not burdensome. Christ's yoke is easy and His burden light (1 Jn. 5: 3; Mt. 11: 30). Do not let us lay upon ourselves or others any other burden beyond His. The Pharisees did exactly this. They added their own traditions to God's commandments. They bound "heavy burdens, hard to bear", and laid them "on men's shoulders" (Mk. 7: 8-13; Mt. 23: 4). Let us not be found emulating these blind leaders of the blind! The Christian must not play the Pharisee. Let us hold fast what we have, that is, what has been given us in the apostolic teaching now recorded in Scripture. Many times the apostles tell us to do just this, to "let what you heard from the beginning abide in you" to "stand firm and hold to the traditions which you were taught by us, either by word of mouth or by letter" and "to live according to Scripture" (1 Jn. 2: 24; 2 Thess. 2: 15; 1 Cor. 4: 6). The Holy Scriptures are themselves a "canon", a yardstick by which to measure and a criterion by which to test. They are an adequate guide and a sufficient rule both of faith and life. Let us hold fast to them, and lay upon ourselves no other burden than is given us by them.

(4) CHRIST'S PROMISE TO THE CONQUEROR

This letter like all the others concludes with gracious promises to the conqueror. Indeed, in this case the conqueror is clearly defined. He is the one who obeys the moral law of Christ. *He who conquers* is, in the language of Christ here, the same as *he who keeps my works until the end* (v. 26). There are several references in this epistle to "works", the works by which we cannot be justified but by which we shall certainly be judged (v. 23). Works are never the ground or means of our salvation, but they are the evidence of it, and therefore they constitute an excellent basis for judgment. Christ speaks in this epistle of *your works* (vv. 19, 23), of *her works* (v. 22 A.V.), and of *my works* (v. 26). His desire is that our works shall ever be patterned after the example of Himself rather than of Jezebel and her tribe, so that we may be said to keep "His" rather than "her" works *until the end*.

To him who conquers in the fight by keeping Christ's works steadfast to the end, He makes two wonderful promises. Here they are in full. *I will give him power over the nations, and he shall rule them with a rod of iron, as when earthen pots are broken in pieces, even as I myself have received power from my Father; and I will give him the morning star* (vv. 26-28). The words *I will give* are quoted twice (vv. 26 and 28), and echo the same phrase in verse 23. If Christ will give to the sinner as his works deserve, He will give to the conqueror far beyond what his works ever could begin to deserve. Christ promised to give the conqueror *power over the nations* and *the morning star*, which expressions convey the notions of authority and revelation.

The first promise borrows its imagery from Psalm 2: 8-9 where the Messiah's future sovereignty over the heathen is remarkably prophesied: "Ask of me", says God to His Christ, "and I will make the nations your heritage, and the ends of the earth your possession. You shall break them with a rod of iron, and dash them in pieces like a potter's vessel" (cf. Rev. 12: 5;

19: 15). This authority Christ now shares with His faithful, conquering people. *Even as I myself have received power from my Father* (v. 27), He says, so I will give power to you. The quotation from Psalm 2 is slightly modified and adapted. The Greek word for to "rule" in verse 27 means literally to "tend". The potter has become a shepherd, and the nations will not only be earthen pots to be smashed in pieces, but sheep to be ruled and disciplined in justice. Exactly how the conqueror will be permitted to share in Christ's reign is beyond our present state of knowledge. It is enough to remind ourselves that Scripture contains many indications that heaven will be for the believer a place not only of privilege but of responsibility. The "good and faithful servant" who has been "faithful over a little" will be "set . . . over much" and will be allowed to "enter into the joy of" his Master. Similarly, to the good servant in the Parable of the Pounds the nobleman says: "Because you have been faithful in a very little, you shall have authority over ten cities". And Paul adds to the Corinthians: "Do you not know that the saints will judge the world?" (Mt. 25: 21, 23; Lk. 19: 17; 1 Cor. 6: 2). It seems fitting that it should be so. He who has learned to keep Christ's works in this life will continue to do them in the next. He who has come to rule his own passions on earth will rule over people in heaven. He who has allowed Christ's Kingdom to be set up in his heart undisputed will share in its further sway beyond this age.

The second promise of Christ to the conqueror concerns His gift of *the morning star* (v. 28). Many suggestions have been made for the elucidation of this phrase, but as always the word of God is its own best interpreter. In Revelation 22: 16 the Lord Jesus describes Himself as "the bright morning star". He is the "star . . . out of Jacob" prophesied by Balaam and "the dayspring from on high" who "hath visited us, to give light to them that sit in darkness and in the shadow of death" (Num. 24: 17; Lk. 1: 78, 79 A.V.). The churches may be "lampstands" and the churches' angels may be described as "stars", but Christ is the bright morning star from whom they derive their light. In pledging this star to the conqueror, then, Christ is but pledging Himself. The faithful Christian who has repudiated the standards of the world, controlled the desires of the flesh and resisted the allurements of the devil will gain this bright morning star. Rejecting Jezebel, he will receive Christ. He will be permitted to share not only in Christ's authority but in Christ's glory. He will not only rule the nations, but possess the Lord of the nations. Refusing to dive into the depths of Satan, he will fathom the depths of Christ. Turning his back on the darkness of sin, he will see the light of the glory of God in the matchless face of Jesus Christ, and the Christian conqueror, however great his renunciations may have been on earth in the battle for holiness, will with this star, this Christ, remain absolutely and eternally content.

> *"You have the name of being alive, and*
> *you are dead"*   Rev. 3: 1

6

THE LETTER TO SARDIS: REALITY
(Rev. 3: 1-6)

*A*ND to the angel of the church in Sardis write: "The words of
him who has the seven spirits of God and the seven stars. I know
your works; you have the name of being alive, and you are dead.
Awake, and strengthen what remains and is on the point of death, for
I have not found your works perfect in the sight of my God. Remember
then what you received and heard; keep that, and repent. If you will
not awake, I will come like a thief, and you will not know at what
hour I will come upon you. Yet you have still a few names in Sardis,
people who have not soiled their garments; and they shall walk with
me in white, for they are worthy. He who conquers shall be clad
thus in white garments, and I will not blot his name out of the
book of life; I will confess his name before my Father and before his
angels. He who has an ear, let him hear what the Spirit says to the
churches."*

The town of Sardis lay about thirty miles south-east of Thyatira
and fifty miles due east of Smyrna. Situated at the foot of
Mount Tmolus and in the fertile valley of the River Hermus,
it was also the converging point of several inland roads, so that
it became a fairly busy centre of trade and traffic. But its ancient
history was more distinguished than its modern. The capital
of the old kingdom of Lydia, it was here that the fabulous Croesus
reigned amid his treasures until it fell to the swift attack of the
Persian conqueror, Cyrus. Later in its history, it had the distinc-

tion of being captured by both Alexander the Great and Antiochus the Great. But it gradually fell on evil days and lost its earlier renown, until in A.D. 17 it was devastated by an earthquake. Through the munificence of the Emperor Tiberius, who remitted its taxes for five years, it was rebuilt, and flourished again to the extent that Strabo could call it "a great city", but it never regained its former glory.

Nothing is known of the origins of the church in Sardis, nor of its early growth, except what may be gathered from this epistle. It is interesting to note that one of its early bishops, towards the end of the second century, Melito by name, is the first known commentator on the Revelation.

The epistle which the risen Jesus dictated to John for transmission to the church of Sardis is one of the most severe of the seven. Its criticism is almost unrelieved. "Like the city itself", remarks R. H. Charles (p. 78), "the church had belied its early promise. Its religious history, like its civil, belonged to the past". We must consider Christ's message to this church.

(1) THE REBUKE CHRIST ADMINISTERS

Only a few simple words were needed by which to expose this church's spiritual bankruptcy, but they were as devastating as the earthquake of A.D. 17: *I know your works; you have the name of being alive, and you are dead* (v. 1). The church of Sardis had acquired a name. Its reputation as a progressive church had evidently spread far and wide. It was well regarded in the city and in the neighbourhood. It was known by the other six churches in the province for its vitality. No false doctrine was taking root in its fellowship. We hear of neither Balaam, nor Nicolaitans, nor Jezebel. "What a live church you have in Sardis!" visitors would exclaim with admiration when they attended its services or watched its activities; and so no doubt it appeared. I dare say its congregation was quite large for those days, and was growing and even fashionable. Its programme included many excellent projects. It was positively humming with activity. There was no shortage in the church of money or talent or manpower. There was every indication of life and vigour.

But outward appearances are notoriously deceptive; and this socially distinguished congregation was a spiritual graveyard. It seemed to be alive, but it was actually dead. It had a name for virility, but it had no right to its name. Its works were beautiful graveclothes which were but a thin disguise for this ecclesiastical corpse. The eyes of Christ saw beyond the clothes to the skeleton. It was dead as mutton. It even stank. To use Christ's own words to enlarge on this church's dead condition, *I have not found your works perfect in the sight of my God* (v. 2). There were works done in the church, but they were not "perfect". The word literally means "fulfilled". They were an empty shell, with no body to fill them. They were a routine of duties, but they did not begin to fulfil God's purpose or pattern. The "name" that Sardis had acquired was a name with men, but not with God. It was *before my God*, Christ said, that He had found this church's works deficient. They seemed solid and worthy enough to onlookers, but in the sight of God were thoroughly defective. How badly we need to hear this word of God today! As Christians, we have indeed responsibilities to our fellowmen, but our chief responsibility is to God. It is unto Him that we live, before Him that we stand, and to Him that one day we must give an account. Then let us not rate too highly the opinions of the world or even of the Church. Some Christians grow too depressed when criticized and too elated when flattered. We need to remember that "the LORD sees not as man sees; man looks on the outward appearance, but the LORD looks on the heart" (1 Sam. 16: 7). He looks beneath the surface. He can survey our motives and thoughts and desires. He can see how much reality there is behind our professions, how much life behind our facade.

Another hint is given in the letter to clarify what is meant by the spiritual death which had overtaken Sardis. It is this. The few who did not share in the general stagnation are described as *people who have not soiled their garments* (v. 4). So this death was dirt. Sin had crept into the church, less openly than in the case of the Jezebel party at Thyatira, but its defiling influence had not been missed by the holy eyes of Christ. Beneath the pious exterior of that respectable congregation was secret un- cleanness. Such spiritual defilement is spiritual death. The inhabitants of Sardis, according to Herodotus, had over the course of many years acquired a reputation for lax moral standards and even open licentiousness. Perhaps the church in Sardis had forgotten Paul's injunction "Do not be conformed to this world" or John's "Do not love the world or the things in the world" (Rom. 12: 2; 1 Jn. 2: 15). It may be that gradually, even imperceptibly, the leaven of wickedness and worldliness had spread in the dough, until the whole lump had become vitiated by its influence.

So the name of Sardis was a lie. Indeed, Sardis may be said to be the first church in the history of Christendom to have been well-nigh filled with what we now call "nominal Christians". They were nominally Christ's, but not actually. They had a name for having been quickened, but were still dead. It is a terrible thing to be physically alive and at the same time spiritually dead. Yet Jesus Himself recognized the grim possibility. It was "the dead" whom he expected to "bury their dead". That is, in face of the urgent need at that moment for preaching the gospel, the spiritually dead could attend to the matter of burying the physically dead. St. Paul used the same expression when describing unbelievers, who have not yet received new life in Jesus Christ, as "dead in trespasses and sins". He designated a loose-living woman as being "dead even while she lives", and Jesus knew that nothing but His own lifegiving voice could awaken such dead people and call them forth from their spiritual graves (Mt. 8: 22; Lk. 9: 60; Eph. 2: 1; 1 Tim. 5: 6; Jn. 5: 25).

Now reality is another *sine qua non* of a true church. A church should not only have *the name of being alive* (v. 1) but the life itself. So we must recognize the difference between outward appearance and inward reality. The Bible devotes many pages to this fundamental theme. Was it not this which Amos, Isaiah, Jeremiah and some others among the great eighth and seventh century prophets were at pains to teach Israel and Judah? The courts of the temple and the precincts of the high places teemed with dutiful worshippers. Incense and sacrifices and the noise of melody were being offered to God with punctilious devotion. But, as the Lord Himself said through the prophet Isaiah: "This people draws near with their mouth, and honours me with their lips, while their hearts are far from me" (Is. 29: 13).

It was this very saying that Jesus quoted against the Pharisees, whom He criticized as the successors of those who had rejected and killed the prophets. They gave alms and said prayers and disfigured their faces to fast, in order that it might appear to men that they were giving and praying and fasting. Indeed, He said, they did all their deeds to be seen by men. This unreality Jesus almost savagely condemned. "Woe to you, scribes and Pharisees, hypocrites! for you are like white-washed tombs, which outwardly appear beautiful, but within they are full of dead men's bones and all uncleanness. So you also outwardly appear righteous to men, but within you are full of hypocrisy and iniquity" (Mt. 6: 1-6, 16-18; 23: 5, 27, 28). Evidently Timothy had come across the same spiritual phenomenon in Ephesus, for Paul wrote to him about some who were "holding the form of religion but denying the power of it" (2 Tim. 3: 5). So we trace this ugly tendency right through the Bible, in both the Old Testament and the New. It is a tendency to form without power, a name without life, an outward appearance without an inward reality.

Now the correct word for this behaviour is hypocrisy. It is a Greek word in origin and meant literally to play a part on a stage, or to act in a drama. So hypocrisy is makebelieve, to assume a rôle which is not real. It is the "let's pretend" of religion.

And hypocrisy can permeate the whole life of a church. It can invade our worship. We can have a fine choir, an expensive organ, good music, great anthems and fine congregational singing. We can mouth hymns and psalms with unimpeachable elegance, while our mind wanders and our heart is far from God. We can have pomp and ceremony, colour and ritual, liturgical exactness and ecclesiastical splendour, and yet be offering a worship which is not perfect or "fulfilled" in the sight of God. Those of us whose privilege it is to be in the ordained ministry can be hypocrites in our praying and preaching too. We can lead the prayers in such a perfunctory manner that the congregation never reach the throne of grace, and we can preach rather to display our learning or eloquence than to exalt Christ and bring glory to Him. A torrent of words can pour from our lips, while there is neither sincerity nor power in them. Our Christian service outside church can be contaminated by the same poison. Activity with no inner love for God or man is a hollow mockery and an empty pantomime.

We must turn now, with some relief, from the rebuke Christ administered to hypocritical Sardis, to the remedy He proposed to them.

(2) THE REMEDY CHRIST PROPOSES

What could be done for a dead church like the church in Sardis? The risen Jesus addresses to this church a series of urgent commands. *Awake, and strengthen what remains and is on the point of death . . . Remember then what you received and heard; keep that, and repent* (vv. 2-3). Here are five staccato imperatives: Awake! Strengthen what remains! Remember! Keep that! Repent! These orders fall into two parts. The church of Sardis is instructed first to awake and strengthen what remains, and next to remember its heritage, keep it and repent.

First, *awake, and strengthen what remains and is on the point of death* (v. 2). It is heartening to note that even in dead or moribund Sardis there were some Christians who were not suffering from the general decay. So Christ continues: *Yet you have still a few names in Sardis, people who have not soiled their garments* (v. 4). In that putrefying church there was still a minority which was both alive and kicking. In the sultry torpor of Sardis a fresh breath of lifegiving air from the Holy Spirit could be felt. In the stillness of spiritual stagnation a few ripples could be seen. Within that worldly congregation a godly remnant was left.

It has always been so. When "the Lord saw that the wickedness of man was great in the earth, and that every imagination of the thoughts of his heart was only evil continually" and He resolved to destroy the inhabitants of the earth by a flood, Noah and his family yet found favour in His sight and were spared. Again, when "the Lord rained on Sodom and Gomorrah brimstone and fire from the Lord out of heaven and He overthrew those cities" because of their appalling immorality, "He rescued righteous Lot, greatly distressed by the licentiousness of the wicked". If the whole nation of Israel seemed in the days of Ahab and Jezebel to have forsaken Jehovah and turned to Baal, God could reassure Elijah the prophet that there were still "seven thousand in Israel, all the knees that have not bowed to Baal, and every mouth that has not kissed him". A century later the southern kingdom of Judah was equally unfaithful to the Lord. Divine judgment brought the nation to the verge of extinction as the countryside was laid waste by invading armies: "Except the LORD of hosts had left unto us a very small remnant, we should have been as Sodom, and we should have been like unto Gomorrah". After the exile which the prophet predicted only a remnant, repentant and purified, would return, for, said God: "Though your people Israel be as the sand of the sea, only a remnant of them will return". The tree of Israel would be felled, and the "holy seed" would remain like a stump. So central was this truth to the message of Isaiah that he named one of his sons Shearjashub, which means "A remnant shall return". (Gen. 6: 5-18; 19: 24, 25; 2 Pet. 2: 7; 1 Kings 19: 18; Is. 1: 9 A.V.; 10: 20-22; 6: 13; 7: 3.)

When we reach the New Testament, and the Christian Church is founded, we find that the new Israel also will be but a small remnant. Jesus Himself seems to have clearly anticipated this. His followers must not be ashamed of Him "in this adulterous and sinful generation", He said. They were only a "little flock", but they need not fear, even if when the Son of man comes He will scarcely "find faith on earth" (Mk. 8: 38; Lk. 12: 32; 18: 8).

To return to Sardis, there were in that city a few Christians who were still loyal in heart and mind to Jesus and formed a godly remnant. Though the church's name for vigour was deceitful, there were *a few names* (v. 4) which were true. No stigma attached to them. It is to them, therefore, that Christ brings this stirring exhortation to *awake, and strengthen what remains and is on the point of death*. The metaphor has changed from death to sleep. You cannot appeal to a dead man to wake up! But some church members at Sardis were sleepy rather than dead, and the risen Jesus calls to them to rouse themselves from their heavy slumbers and to be watchful. Several times when He walked this earth, He told His followers to watch. It was a word often on His lips. His disciples must watch and pray; they must let their loins be girded and their lamps burning, and be like men who are waiting for their master to come home from the marriage feast. "Blessed are those servants", He added, "whom the master finds awake when he comes" (Lk. 12: 35-37). Some commentators have suggested that this command to be watchful was particularly appropriate to Sardis because this almost impregnable city had twice fallen to surprise attacks, the first time to the Persian Cyrus, and the second to Antiochus the Great. "Through the failure to watch, . . . the acropolis had been successfully scaled in 549 B.C. by a Median soldier, and in 218 by a Cretan" (*The International Standard Bible Encyclopaedia* p. 2692; article "Sardis").

Once awake again, the living remnant of the church were to

strengthen what remains. Professor Swete points out that the Greek word here used for to strengthen was "a technical word in primitive pastoralia" (p. 48). We read of the apostle Paul returning to Galatia on his third missionary journey, "strengthening the disciples" whom his early preaching and teaching had brought to Christ. He writes to the Roman Christians that he longs to visit them and "strengthen" them in their Christian faith (Acts 18: 23; Rom. 1: 11). Peter and James use the same word in their epistles. New Christians are weak; they need to be strengthened. They are but babes in Christ; they need to be nurtured and loved. They are often wobbly, and need to be established. Older, maturer Christians have a great responsibility in the congregation to younger ones. Stronger Christians must not despise the weak, but encourage and strengthen them by their example, their teaching and their friendship.

Here then is the duty of the Church within the church. God has often worked through minorities. It is His gracious plan to call out from the world and even from the masses of nominal believers a faithful and committed remnant to be His instrument. An alive and awake minority can recall the majority from death. A robust remnant can *strengthen what remains and is on the point of death.*

Do you belong to what is sometimes called "a dead church", and you are tempted to leave it and to go elsewhere? Why not heed this word of Christ? Let the revived Christians come together to pray and to wait upon God. A dynamic minority of living and awakened Christians can by prayer and love preserve a dying church from utter extinction.

If you will not awake, Christ adds, *I will come like a thief, and you will not know at what hour I will come upon you* (v. 3). Jesus had often issued the warning that His final coming would be as stealthy and unexpected as a burglar's. This special coming too, in judgment upon an individual church, would be un-heralded. As the robbers, who lurked in caves in the mountains above Sardis, suddenly swooped upon the unwary, so Christ would come. The church's lampstand would be removed; its life would be smothered; and its light finally extinguished.

The second set of divine commands to the church in Sardis was: *Remember then what you received and heard; keep that, and repent* (v. 3). The ascended Lord had told the church of Ephesus to remember (2: 5). The Sardian church is told to remember too. Memory is a precious and blessed gift. Nothing can stab the conscience so wide awake as memories of the past. The shortest road to repentance is remembrance. Let a man once recall what he used to be and reflect on what by God's grace he could be, and he will be led to repent, turning back from his sin to his Saviour. Moreover, what is true of the individual Christian is true of the local church as a whole. Some churches which today are dead or dying can look back on a long and glorious history. Their older members can call to mind the former days when the congregation was a living fellowship of active workers and souls were being regularly added to their number. Let past history challenge us to present endeavour!

But we must be a little more precise. *Remember then what you received and heard; keep that* . . . (v. 3). We must investigate these words "what" and "that". Exactly what is it to which Christ refers? What had they received and heard which they were to remember? Was it simply the word of God, the gospel? I think not. Sound doctrine alone cannot reclaim a church from death. Orthodoxy can sometimes itself be dead. They had received more than the gospel. They had received the Holy Spirit. He is the great gift that men and women receive when they respond to the gospel with the hearing of faith and obedience. "Receive the Holy Spirit" said Jesus to the disciples on Easter Day when He breathed on them in anticipation of Pentecost. "Repent, and be baptized every one of you in the name of Jesus Christ for the forgiveness of sins", cried Peter when the Day of Pentecost came, adding: "and you shall receive the gift of the Holy Spirit". St. Paul knew also that this gift of the Spirit was the heavenly birthright of every child of God. "Did you receive the Holy Spirit when you believed?" he asked some disciples in Ephesus, clearly expecting an affirmative answer. "The world cannot receive" Him, but every Christian "receives the Spirit . . . by hearing with faith", and "any one who does not have the Spirit of Christ does not belong to Him" (Jn. 20: 22; Acts 2: 38; 19: 2; Jn. 14: 17; Gal. 3: 2; Rom. 8: 9).

God gives the Spirit; man receives Him. Indeed, the greatest gift the Christian has ever received, ever will or could receive, is the Spirit of God Himself. He can enter the sanctuary of the soul. He can come into the inner shrine of the human personality and remake us from within. He can be an indwelling, abiding presence to fill us with love, joy and peace; to subdue our passions and transform our characters; and to change us into the image of Christ. Today God has no temple made with hands. His dwellingplace is His people. He inhabits both the individual believer and the local Christian community. Indeed, in the very same epistle in which the apostle Paul asks: "Do you not know that your body is a temple of the Holy Spirit within you?" he adds "Do you not know that you (plural, corporately) are God's temple, and that God's Spirit dwells in you?" (Gal. 5: 22, 23, 16; 2 Cor 3: 18; 1 Cor. 6: 19; 3: 16).

It may well be then that Christ is referring to the Holy Spirit when He commands the Christians of Sardis: *Remember then what you received* (v. 3). That this is the right interpretation is suggested by the first verse of the epistle. Here Christ describes Himself as the One *who has the seven spirits of God and the seven stars* (v. 1). In every epistle the introductory description which He gives of Himself is suited to the condition of the particular church addressed. There is no reason to suppose that the letter to Sardis is an exception to this rule. It is the church which needs to learn that the ascended Lord has both *the seven spirits* and *the seven stars*. The seven stars are "the angels" of the seven churches. Whether these angels are the churches' presiding ministers or heavenly representatives, they stand for the churches.

But what or who are *the seven spirits of God*? The expression is admittedly strange, and yet there can be little doubt that it denotes none other than the Holy Spirit Himself, the third Person of the Trinity. This can be deduced from the first occurrence of the phrase in 1: 4 where grace and peace are desired for the seven churches of Asia "from Him who is and who was and who is to come, and from the seven spirits who are before His throne, and from Jesus Christ. . . ." Here the seven spirits are linked with the Eternal Father and with Jesus Christ as the single source of both grace and peace. The closeness of these seven spirits to the throne (4: 5), and their intimate relation to Jesus Christ (5: 6) suggest the same conclusion that they are the Holy Spirit.

Why then is the expression "seven spirits" used when the Holy Spirit is one person in the Godhead? It will be sufficient to answer with Archbishop Trench "that He is regarded here not so much in His personal unity as in His manifold energies" (p. 9).

So Jesus reminds the church of Sardis that He has "the seven spirits". Christ has the Holy Spirit. The Holy Spirit is the Spirit of Christ. Eternally He proceeds from the Son as well as from the Father, as the Western Church has always believed. Historically, He was sent or "poured out" by Christ on the Day of Pentecost, as the Bible explicitly states (Rom. 8: 9; Acts 2: 33).

Now this Spirit of Christ is "the Spirit of Life" (Rom. 8: 2). As the Nicene Creed declares, He is both "the Lord" and "the Lifegiver". What other message does a dead or moribund church need to hear? It is the Holy Spirit who can breathe into our formal worship until it comes alive and is real. It is He who can animate our dead works and make them pulsate with life. He can rescue a dying church and make it a living force in the community. Let Him once fill us with His vital presence, and our work, worship and witness will become marvellously transformed. The word of God tells us that we must pray in the Spirit, preach in the Spirit, worship in the Spirit, live in the Spirit and walk in the Spirit (Jude 20; 1 Thess. 1: 5; Jn. 4: 24

and Phil. 3: 3; Gal. 5: 25, 16). A stale church can be freshened by Him and a sleepy church awakened. He can strengthen a weak church, and quicken one that is dead.

Let us not miss the fact that the Christ who has the seven spirits also has the seven stars. Indeed, "the 'spirits' are seven", suggests Swete, "because the churches in which they operate are seven" (p. 6). The seven stars, standing in some way for the churches, are in His right hand (1: 16, 20). Are the seven spirits in His left? If only He were to bring His hands together! If only the Spirit were to fill the Church! Christ is willing. Did He not pour out His Spirit upon His Church on the Day of Pentecost? The Holy Spirit has been given to the Church once and for all, and is adequate for all the Church's needs. He can never be "poured out" again. There can be no repetition of the Day of Pentecost. When He came, He came to stay with us for ever (Jn. 14: 16). But although He will never withdraw His presence altogether, He can be "grieved" and even "quenched" (Eph. 4: 30; 1 Thess. 5: 19).

Perhaps then there is no more urgent message for twentieth-century Christians than this: "Be filled with the Spirit" (Eph. 5: 18). He dwells within you; but does He fill you? You possess Him; but does He possess you? If we would but submit to His sovereign will in daily obedience, and claim His continuous fulness by faith, our Christian life would be lifted to a higher plane and our church life revolutionized. Not that we can press a button and settle this matter for good. The fulness of the Holy Spirit is an experience to be maintained. It may be lost. In St. Paul's command to us to be filled, the verb is a present imperative passive. It means "go on being filled", or even "be in the state of being filled". Every day we must renew our repentance and obedience and by faith receive His filling, until we live continuously in an attitude of humble, empty dependence on Him. Only so can Christ's Church be a living Church. We spend much time planning, but little time praying. We work for God, but seldom wait on God. We think and scheme and organize. We administer great projects and create impressive committees. But we often leave the Holy Spirit out. He has rightly been called the forgotten member of the Trinity. Only when the Church of Christ is filled with the Spirit of Christ can spiritual death be banished and a name for life have any reality behind it.

> O Breath of Life, come sweeping through us,
>   Revive Thy Church with life and power;
> O Breath of Life, come, cleanse, renew us
>   And fit Thy Church to meet this hour.

(3) THE REWARD CHRIST PROMISES

Once again the epistle ends with a promise to the conqueror; and once again the reward promised is appropriate to the church. What Christ offered Sardis concerned their garments and their name. Some had soiled their garments; the conqueror would be clothed in white. Some had received a lying name; the conqueror's name would be honoured in heaven.

Firstly, *they shall walk with me in white, for they are worthy. He who conquers shall be clad thus in white garments* (vv. 4-5). Many in Sardis had *soiled their garments* (v. 4), with the dirt of sin, but those who had resisted the evil allurements of the world would wear white raiment and enjoy fellowship with Christ in heaven. Whiteness is a popular colour in this book. We read of a white stone and a white cloud, of white horses and a great white throne (2: 17; 14: 14; 19: 11, 14; 20: 11). "'White' is everywhere the colour and livery of heaven" (Trench p. 126). Whether or not it stands also for festivity and victory, or has any reference to the use of a white toga by the Romans, it certainly symbolizes purity. Of those who are clothed in white, it is written: *they are worthy* (v. 4). Not, however, that the conqueror earns his reward by right, since his forgiveness and moral strength are due to the free grace of Christ alone. No.

His worthiness is borrowed from Christ. The only way to be made fit for entry into God's Kingdom is to be cleansed by Christ who died for us, or, in the rich imagery of this book, to wash our robes and make them white in the blood of the Lamb (7: 14; cf. 22: 14).

Secondly, *I will not blot his name out of the book of life; I will confess his name before my Father and before His angels* (v. 5). The Scriptures tell us that God has a book. Of course it is only a symbol; but behind the symbol is a solemn truth. God keeps, as it were, a register in heaven, in which the names of His people are enrolled. It is called "God's book", and "the Book of the Living", since the names of the spiritually dead are not found in it. It is also a "Book of Remembrance", containing the names of those who "fear the Lord and think on His name". Sometimes it is just "the Book", but more often "the Book of Life" or "the Lamb's Book of Life" (Ex. 32: 32, 33; Ps. 69: 28; Mal. 3: 16; Dan. 12: 1, Phil. 4: 3 and Rev. 20: 15; Rev. 13: 8 and 21: 27). One day the books will be opened, and the dead will be judged by what is written in the books, and everyone whose name is not found written in the Book of Life will be "thrown into the lake of fire" (Rev. 20: 11-15).

Is your name written in the Lamb's book of life? You can have a name among men for being alive (like the church of Sardis) and still have no entry in God's book of the living. Your name can be on a church register without being on the Divine Register. You can have your name placed on the Electoral Roll of a church and not be among those who have been enrolled in heaven. Your name can be included in the baptism, confirmation and wedding registers of a church and yet be missing from the book of life. Jesus told His disciples to rejoice that their names were "written in heaven" (Lk. 10: 20; cf. Heb. 12: 23). Can you rejoice like that today?

Christ's gracious promise to the Christian conqueror in Sardis is that He will not blot his name out of the book. The Greek sentence has a double negative, as if Jesus meant: "I will never by any means blot out his name". Indeed, far from removing the conqueror's name from the register of heaven, Christ promises to confess it before His Father and the angels. This is but a repetition of what He had said in the days of His flesh. "Every one who acknowledges me before men, I also will acknowledge before my Father who is in heaven" and "before the angels of God" (Mt. 10: 32; Lk. 12: 8).

So the epistle closes. We can only hope that the church of Sardis heeded this moving message. If they did not, we must. The time is too short for us to play the hypocrite. The needs of the world are so great that we cannot afford to dabble in religion or trifle with God. To be given by men a name for life is not enough; we must possess an inward reality and purity which are known and pleasing to God. We must neither soil our garments nor betray our name. Filled with the living Spirit of Christ, we can conquer. Then at last we shall wear white raiment and walk with Christ in heaven; and our names, indelibly inscribed in the Book of Life, will be acknowledged before God and the angels.

> Come, Holy Ghost, our souls inspire,
>   And lighten with celestial fire;
> Thou the anointing Spirit art,
>   Who dost Thy sevenfold gifts impart.
>
> Thy blessed unction from above
>   Is comfort, life, and fire of love;
> Enable with perpetual light
>   The dullness of our blinded sight.

> *"Behold, I have set before you an open door"*
>
> Rev. 3: 8

7

THE LETTER
TO PHILADELPHIA: OPPORTUNITY
(Rev. 3: 7-13)

*A*ND *to the angel of the church in Philadelphia write: "The words of the holy one, the true one, who has the key of David, who opens and no one shall shut, who shuts and no one opens. I know your works. Behold, I have set before you an open door, which no one is able to shut; I know that you have but little power, and yet you have kept my word and have not denied my name. Behold, I will make those of the synagogue of Satan who say that they are Jews and are not, but lie—behold, I will make them come and bow down before your feet, and learn that I have loved you. Because you have kept my word of patient endurance, I will keep you from the hour of trial which is coming on the whole world, to try those who dwell upon the earth. I am coming soon; hold fast what you have, so that no one may seize your crown. He who conquers, I will make him a pillar in the temple of my God; never shall he go out of it, and I will write on him the name of my God, and the name of the city of my God, the New Jerusalem which comes down from my God out of heaven, and my own new name. He who has an ear, let him hear what the Spirit says to the churches."*

The town of Philadelphia was situated about twenty-eight miles south-east of Sardis and was the next town which the postman would reach on his circular tour of the seven churches of Asia. Like Sardis it was in the fertile region of Lydia and was dominated by Mount Tmolus. It stood on the banks of the river Cogamus, an insignificant tributary of the Hermus. The district was dangerously volcanic. Strabo called Philadelphia "a city full of earthquakes". Earth tremors were frequent, and had caused many former inhabitants to leave the city for a safer home. The severe earthquake of A.D. 17 which devastated Sardis almost completely demolished Philadelphia.

But by the nineties Philadelphia, with the aid of an imperial subsidy, had been completely rebuilt, and within the city was a church of Jesus Christ. To it the sixth of the seven letters is addressed, in which the ascended Christ expresses warm approval of His people. The previous letter to Sardis contained almost unmitigated censure. The letter to Philadelphia is one of almost unqualified commendation. *I know your works* (v. 8), He begins, as in each epistle, and continues a little later: *you have kept my word and have not denied my name* (v. 8). Again, *you have kept my word of patient endurance* (v. 10). Evidently, there had been some recent persecution in Philadelphia, but the Christians (though hard pressed) had held fast their profession. As in Pergamum, where Antipas had been cruelly martyred, so in Philadelphia the Christians had manfully stood their ground (cf. 2: 13). They were patiently bearing tribulation and shame for Christ's sake. In Jesus Christ they were sharing with the exiled John "the tribulation and the kingdom and the patient endurance" (1: 9).

This letter to the Philadelphian church is particularly striking on account of the vivid symbolical descriptions which it includes. In it we read of a key, a door and a pillar. The church is described as having set before it *an open door, which no one is able to shut* (v. 8); Christ is described as the One *who has the key of David* (v. 7); while the conqueror is described as being made a *pillar in the temple of . . . God* (v. 12). We must consider carefully the exciting relation which exists between the church's open door, Christ's master key and the pillar in heaven.

(1) THE CHURCH AND THE OPEN DOOR

Behold, says Jesus, *I have set before you an open door, which no one is able to shut* (v. 8). What is this wide open door which nobody can shut? Well, the idea of doors is a fairly common one in the pages of the Bible. An open door is a door of opportunity. When the door is closed, the opportunity has passed. The metaphor is used in Scripture in two main senses.

The first open door is the opportunity of salvation. Some commentators think this is the meaning in the Philadelphian letter. The suggestion is unlikely. But the picture is so clear in other parts of the Bible that we can scarcely omit it. Jesus Himself twice used this language. One of these occasions was during the Sermon on the Mount. This is what He said: "Enter by the narrow gate; for the gate is wide and the way is easy, that leads to destruction, and those who enter by it are many. For the gate is narrow and the way is hard, that leads to life, and those who find it are few" (Mt. 7: 13, 14).

Here are two gates, and both are open. One door opens onto a broad and crowded thoroughfare. The road slopes gently downward and ends in the destruction called hell. The other door opens onto a sparsely populated and narrow path, which winds steeply upward and leads to life in the city of God.

Let us look more closely at the words of Jesus. He contrasted not only two ways and two ends, but two gates. Both are open and inviting, but one is wide and the other narrow. The wide gate is so spacious that it is easy for carefree people to surge through it in their crowds. But the other gate is so low that we must stoop humbly and cannot enter it proudly erect; and so narrow that we must go in one at a time and then can only just squeeze through. There is no room to take anything with us. Our sins and our selfishness—yes and even the ragged bundles of our own morality—must all be left behind.

Let me repeat what Christ taught. Although one door is wide and the other low and narrow, and although many are thronging through the one, while a few slip quietly through the other, both doors stand open. Which have you entered?

The second open door is the opportunity of service. This is very important. Many ignorant and thoughtless folk think that Christians are a bunch of self-satisfied prigs who are concerned only to save their own skins. They enter the open door (our critics continue) and sit down comfily in the luxurious halls of salvation. They lick their lips and fold their arms in complacency. They gloat over their own safety and care not a tinker's cuss for anybody else.

What an appalling caricature of Christians this is! If anybody exists who really thinks and behaves in such a manner, it is safe to say that he or she is not a Christian. Mark Guy Pearce spoke a wise and true word when he said: "Unless a man's faith saves him out of selfishness into service, it will certainly never save him out of hell into heaven".

The truth is this. The Christian believer who has received salvation as a free gift from God through Jesus Christ is deeply concerned about the wellbeing, material and spiritual, of his fellow men. Once inside the door of salvation, his eye lights upon another door which stands open before him. It is the door of service. And so, having gone in through the door of salvation, he hurries out through the door of service to look for others and (in the words of Christ) "compel them to come in".

No doubt it is this opportunity of service which is primarily in view in the letter to the Philadelphian church. Openings for the spread of the gospel were many and great in the Roman Empire of the first century A.D. The *pax Romana* permitted Christian evangelists to go about their business with comparative freedom, speaking the common Greek language, treading the fine Roman roads and using as their textbook the Septuagint (Greek) version of the Old Testament. Besides, wherever they went, they found groping minds and hungry hearts. The old pagan superstitions were being abandoned. The Holy Spirit was stirring the thoughts and desires of ordinary men and women.

Many thirsty souls were panting for the water of life. St. Paul found this wherever he went.

On the third of his famous missionary journeys he spent three years in Ephesus, both giving public lectures in a hired hall and visiting people privately in their own homes. Night and day he was busy preaching the gospel. Of this period he wrote: "A wide door for effective work has opened to me" (1 Cor. 16: 9). When later he reached Rome, the capital of the world, and was for two years held a captive in his own hired house, he yet spoke of Christ to all who visited him— Jews, Roman soldiers, and a runaway slave called Onesimus. With all these opportunities he was still not satisfied. "Pray for us also", he wrote to Christian friends in Colosse, "that God may open to us a door for the word, to declare the mystery of Christ on account of which I am in prison, that I may make it clear as I ought to speak" (Col. 4: 3, 4; cf. 2 Cor. 2: 12).

There was a wide-open door in Ephesus, and a half-open door in Rome. In Philadelphia too a door had been opened by Christ. Not that all was easy. As in Ephesus so in Philadelphia, if the door was open there were also "many adversaries" (1 Cor. 16: 9). For one thing, the Philadelphian church was pathetically weak. *I know that you have but little power* (v. 8), says Christ. Perhaps the congregation was small, or perhaps it was composed largely of the lower classes of Roman society. The church did not naturally exert any great influence on the city. But this was not to deter them from evangelism. Next, there was opposition, and, as in Smyrna (2: 9), it appears to have come from the Jewish population of the city. So fanatical was their resistance to the gospel of their Messiah, that they are again called not a synagogue of God but *the synagogue of Satan who say that they are Jews and are not, but lie* (v. 9). I have no doubt that the fierceness of this opposition to the truth tempted the Philadelphian Christians to hold their peace and mind their own business. I dare say there were not lacking in the Philadelphian church those who counselled that discretion was the better part of valour and that Christians should not stir up trouble. But Christ was of another mind. It was in this very city where Jewish antagonism was so strong that He opened a door for the gospel. Indeed, He makes it clear that if only the Christians would boldly march through the door under His banner, some of those who would capitulate would be Jews! *Behold, He promises, I will make those* (literally, some) *of the synagogue of Satan . . . come and bow down before your feet, and learn that I have loved you* (v. 9).

Jewish converts are here portrayed as captives on the battle-field. They themselves would be familiar with this imagery. It had been prophesied of them years before that "the sons of those who oppressed you shall come bending low to you; and all who despised you shall bow down at your feet" (Is. 60: 14). But now the tables are turned. Instead of Gentiles kneeling at Jewish feet, Jews will bow down before Christians—not of course to worship them, but humbly to recognize the Christian Church as the new and the true Israel on whom God has set His love.

The third obstacle in the path of the Philadelphian Christians was the threat of future tribulation. The thunder clouds of persecution were gathering. At any time the storm might break. Surely this was no time for evangelism? This was a time for retrenchment and consolidation, not for advance? Again, Christ has different ideas. He warns them of coming trial with one breath, and with the next urges them to step through the open door without fear. Moreover, He promises *I will keep you from the hour of trial which is coming on the whole world, to try those who dwell upon the earth* (v. 10). Had they kept His word? Then He would keep them. He would not spare them from the suffering; but He would uphold them in it.

How easily do we give up! Subtle and specious are the reasons we find to excuse ourselves the bother of evangelistic endeavour. Our forces are small and feeble, we say. The opposition is great, and the danger of further unpleasantness real. Let us not do anything rash or foolish. Let us wait a while until the circumstances are more propitious. Does not the Bible itself say "There is a time to speak and a time to be silent"? Yes, yes, but the devil himself can misquote and misapply Scripture like that. Neither the Church's weakness nor present nor future opposition should silence us. The Philadelphian church had all these handicaps; yet it was before them that Christ opened the door of service.

He could already say to them: *You have kept my word and have not denied my name* (v. 8). But even this was not enough. To guard the truth and refrain from denying Christ is a poor substitute for aggressive missionary effort! Had they kept Christ's word? Let them now begin to spread it! Had they refused to deny Christ's name? Let them now positively proclaim it!

In what sense Christ had opened a door for the gospel in Philadelphia we cannot say. But perhaps, as some scholars have suggested, the church's peculiar opportunities were due to the city's geographical location. According to Professor William Ramsay, the intention of the city's founder in the second century B.C. had been "to make it a centre of the Graeco-Asiatic civilization and a means of spreading the Greek language and manners in the eastern parts of Lydia and in Phrygia. It was a missionary city from the beginning. . . ." (*The Letters to the Seven Churches of Asia*, pp. 391-2). What the city had been for Greek culture, it was now to be for the Christian gospel. It was built on one of the great Roman roads which thrust its way like an arrow into the heart of the interior. To use Professor Swete's words, Philadelphia was "on the borders of Mysia, Lydia and Phrygia" (p. 53), while Professor Ramsay describes it as being "the keeper of the gateway" to the central plateau and "on the threshold of the eastern country" (Hastings' *Dictionary of the Bible*, III, p. 831). The Philadelphian church seems to have had the chance to spread far and wide the good news of God's grace and Kingdom. The door was open. No man could shut it. Let them pass through!

The same is true of the Christian Church in many parts of the world today. Some doors are closed; but many are open. There are more vacancies for Christians than can be filled, and more opportunities than can be taken. There is a shortage of man-power of the right kind. There is a lack of men and women who are on the one hand trained and competent, and on the other wholly committed to Christ. The Church urgently needs Christians of apostolic zeal who will count all things loss for Christ, and hazard life and career and reputation for Him. The open doors are many; but there are few to go through them.

In the church in central London which it is my privilege to serve, we have a mixed group called "the Philadelphian Fellow-ship". They are a body of Christians who are pledged to seek God's will for their future, to pray regularly that He will disclose it, to prepare themselves for the possibility of whole-time Christian service, and to go anywhere God may later call them. This fellowship has been given the epithet "Philadel-phian" partly because the Greek word *philadelphia* means "brotherly love" and partly because its members are investigating open doors. At present there are fifty-five women and seventeen men in it. One longs for thousands of such "Philadelphians" throughout the Church of Christ.

Here then is the balance of the Christian life. It is a life of give and take. "Freely you have received", said Christ, "freely give". First we take what He offers; then we give what He asks. He sets before us the open doors of salvation and service. He bids us go in through the one to receive salvation and out through the other to give service. Which of these doors have you gone through? It is not possible to go through the second until we have entered the first. Will you come in? and then go out? "I am the door; if anyone enters by me, he will be saved, and will go in and out and find pasture". So "the Lord will keep your going out and your coming in from this time forth and for evermore" (Jn. 10: 9; Ps. 121: 8).

(2) CHRIST AND THE KEY OF DAVID

In telling the Philadelphian church of the open door which He had set before them, Jesus Christ thus significantly begins His letter: *The words of the holy one, the true one, who has the key of David, who opens and no one shall shut, who shuts and no one opens* (v. 7). To begin with, He is selfconsciously divine. "The Holy One" is a title which Jehovah gave Himself in the Old Testament (e.g. Is. 40: 25). Jesus now assumes it naturally and without any fuss. He is not only holy; He is true. He hates all evil and error. He is the perfection of righteousness and the fulfilment of all prophecies. One of the shadowy predictions of the Old Testament which He has fulfilled is mentioned here. It concerns *the key of David* which He claims to possess. We turn in thought from the open door to the key which opened it. The door stands open before the church because its key is in the hand of Christ.

The language is borrowed from Isaiah 22 where it is used of a certain Eliakim. He was one of the three delegates chosen to negotiate for the kingdom of Judah with the Assyrian Rabshakeh. This was doubtless because of the honourable position he occupied in the palace. He had been made steward over King Hezekiah's household. God gave him this authority, calling him "a father to the inhabitants of Jerusalem and to the house of Judah", and added: "I will place on his shoulder the key of the house of David; he shall open, and none shall shut; and he shall shut, and none shall open" (2 Kings 18: 17, 18; Is. 22: 21, 22).

It is not very difficult to see that Eliakim prefigured or fore-shadowed Jesus Christ; for Christ is the head of God's household, the Church. He is the "true" vizier, of whom Eliakim was the prototype, and He was "faithful over God's house". To Him God has given "all authority in heaven and on earth" (Heb. 3: 6; Mt. 28: 18). It is He therefore who has the keys, not only "of Death and Hades" (1: 18) but of salvation and of service. No man can enter until Christ opens the door. Nor can any man enter when He has closed it. Christ says of Himself, as God had said of Eliakim, that He *opens and no one shall shut* and *shuts and no one opens* (v. 7). So, if the door is the symbol of the church's opportunity, the key is the symbol of Christ's authority.

First, Christ holds the key to the door of salvation. Do we wish to enter the narrow door and step onto the narrow way which leads to life? Jesus Christ has the key. None but He can open this door. We may observe that the key is in the hand of Christ, and not in the hand of Peter. Christ certainly said to Peter "I will give you the keys of the kingdom of heaven" (Mt. 16: 19). And Peter used them. By his proclamation of the gospel the first Jews were converted on the day of Pentecost. Through the laying on of his hands (with John) the Holy Spirit was given to the first Samaritan believers; and through his ministry the first Gentile, Cornelius the Roman centurion, was born again and baptized. By the use of the keys committed to him Peter opened the Kingdom of heaven to the first Jews, the first Samaritans and the first Gentiles (Acts 2: 14-41; 8: 14-17; 10: 44-48). But now the keys are back in the hands of Christ, and if men use them at all today it is only in the secondary sense that they are privileged to preach the gospel through which sinners believe and are saved.

The key of salvation is the hand of Christ. Indeed, He has "opened the gate of heaven to all believers". *I have set before you an open door* (v. 8), He says. The tense is perfect. He opened it once long ago. It still stands open today. How is this so? Because at the threshold of the narrow door there stands a cross. On it there hung many centuries past our Saviour. He died for us. He went there for us. He had no sins of His own; He bore our sins in His own body. He did not deserve to die; He took our deserts. He gladly accepted in His own sacred person the judgment our sins had most richly and righteously deserved. That is why the gate is open. Any sinner may enter the inner sanctuary

of God's presence now, and that with confidence, "by the blood
of Jesus, by the new and living way which He opened for us
through the curtain, that is, His flesh" (Heb. 10: 19, 20).

Have you ever entered by this door? Perhaps you have
wandered for many weary years in the meandering bypaths of
aimlessness. Then set your foot on the highway which leads to
glory! Christ is the living one, who died and rose and has the
keys of death. He says *I have set before you an open door, which
no one is able to shut.* No; no man can shut it. But one day it
will be shut. Christ Himself will shut it. The key of Christ
which unlocked it will lock it again. And when He shuts it,
no man can open it. Both admission and exclusion are in His
power alone.

You find this hard to accept? Then listen to Christ's own
words: "Strive to enter by the narrow door; for many, I tell
you, will seek to enter and will not be able. When once the
householder has risen up and shut the door, you will begin to
stand outside and to knock at the door, saying, 'Lord, open to
us.' He will answer you, 'I do not know where you come
from.' Then you will begin to say 'We ate and drank in your
presence, and you taught in our streets.' But he will say, 'I tell
you, I do not know where you come from; depart from me,
all you workers of iniquity!' There you will weep and gnash
your teeth, when you see Abraham and Isaac and Jacob and all
the prophets in the kingdom of God and you yourselves thrust
out" (Lk. 13: 24-28). We may batter at the door and cry "open
to us", but He will reply "I never knew you". We may respond
indignantly "But we ate and drank in Your presence; we took
the bread and sipped the wine at Holy Communion. You
taught us too. We sat in the pews and listened to Your word".
But again He will say "I tell you I do not know where you
come from".

These are solemn words. Let us heed them. I can be a regular
churchgoer, and sit under the sound of the gospel. I can be a
communicant also, and still remain outside the door of salvation.

Then let me enter the door. Let me kneel before the cross. Let me put my trust in Jesus Christ personally as my Saviour. Let me say to Him:

> Just as I am—without one plea
> But that Thy blood was shed for me,
> And that Thou bidd'st me come to Thee,
> O Lamb of God, I come!

Then let me rise to my feet and step quickly through the door before it is too late. Let me be sure that when the door is shut I am on the inside. Jesus gave us another serious warning. He told a story about ten girls. They were wedding attendants who were waiting for the bridegroom to return home after claiming and fetching his bride. Five girls were sensible, and five were stupid. The sensible ones made all necessary preparations. They filled their lamps with oil and were ready. The stupid five made no preparations. Their lamps were empty. Instead of getting busy, they went to sleep. While the bridegroom delayed, there was still time. But when the bridegroom came, it was too late. The sensible five who had got ready went in with the bridegroom and bride to the marriage feast, and the door was shut. The stupid five hurried off to fetch oil, and when at last they came to the feast, they could not get in. They hammered at the door with their fists, and cried "Lord, Lord, open to us". But the bridegroom replied "I do not know you" (Mt. 25: 1-13).

For us the door will be shut either when we die or when Christ returns, whichever is the sooner. Then it will be too late. At present the bridegroom delays. So let us make haste and be ready.

Secondly, Christ holds the key to the door of service. There is little question that the men and women of the Bible had a keener sense than we have of the sovereignty of God in the world. They did not believe that humans had the right to force closed doors and break in. This is plain in both the Old and the New

Testaments. Was it a question of the military career of the Persian conqueror, Cyrus? "Thus says the Lord to His anointed, to Cyrus, whose right hand I have grasped, to subdue nations before him and ungird the loins of kings, to open doors before him that gates may not be closed: 'I will go before you and level the mountains, I will break in pieces the doors of bronze and cut asunder the bars of iron'". Or, was the apostle Peter miraculously released from Herod's prison in answer to the church's prayers so that his chains fell off his hands? Then, led by an angel past the first and second guard, "the iron gate leading into the city . . . opened to them of its own accord". Again, did Paul and Barnabas on the first missionary journey travel over land and sea, hill and dale, mountain and swamp? Were they abused, hated and stoned and yet used to win many for Christ? Then they had an explanation. On their return "they gathered the church together and declared all that God had done with them and how He had opened a door of faith to the Gentiles" (Is. 45: 1, 2; Acts 12: 1-11; 14: 27).

Christ has the keys. He opens the doors. Then let us not barge our way unceremoniously through doors which are still closed. We must wait for Him to make openings for us. Damage is continually being done to the cause of Christ by rude or blatant testimony. It is indeed right to seek to win for Christ our friends and relatives at home and at work. But we are sometimes in a greater hurry than God. Be patient! Pray hard and love much, and wait expectantly for the opportunity of witness. The same applies to our future. More mistakes are probably made by speed than by sloth, by impatience than by dilatoriness. God's purposes often ripen slowly. If the door is shut, don't put your shoulder to it. Wait till Christ takes out the key and opens it.

But of course many doors are already standing wide open. Christ has used His keys. He has turned many locks and drawn many bolts. He has opened many doors, and outside are the millions who still beckon us and say "Come over . . . and help us".

Have we ever heard their appeal? What are we going to do with our life? Are we going to feather our nest with down and line our pockets with gold? Are we bent on making a fortune and retiring young in comfort, having turned a deaf ear and a blind eye to the needs of a world without Christ? Or shall we rather scorn the way of safety and luxury, and hasten through the open doors to the needy multitudes outside?

This was Christ's message to Philadelphia. His words were not addressed to an individual, nor to the ministers, nor to a select circle within the fellowship. He was writing to the whole church. It was before the whole church of Philadelphia that He had opened a door. This is the New Testament ideal. Evangelism is not the prerogative of parsons. It is not the hobby of a few fanatics. It is a duty resting upon the whole congregation and upon every member of it. Every Christian is called to be a witness. Every local Christian community is called to mobilize its forces and marshal them into battle array. How much impact is our local church making on its neighbourhood? Are our church members being trained for active evangelistic enterprise? Are we visiting the homes of the district, teaching the young, preaching in the open air, arranging special services in which the gospel is preached, and aiming to lead our own friends to Christ? These are doors which Christ has opened. We must be sure to go through them. The key is Christ's; but the choice is ours.

(3) THE CONQUEROR AS A PILLAR IN GOD'S TEMPLE

Once more Christ is not content merely to exhort. To His admonitions He adds promises. *I am coming soon*, He says; *hold fast what you have, so that no one may seize your crown* (v. 11). Let the Christians in Philadelphia stand firm as well as move forward. Let no enemy rob them of their crown. Then comes the special pledge to the conqueror. *He who conquers, I will make him a pillar in the temple of my God; never shall he go out of it, and I*

will write on him the name of my God, and the name of the city of
my God, the New Jerusalem which comes down from my God out of
heaven, and my own new name (v. 12). What could be more
appropriate to the active evangelists in Philadelphia? The same
precious promise applies to us. If we renounce in this life the
way of ease, we shall in the next life, in God's temple which is
heaven, be made pillars, stable, immovable, secure, which will
not fall even if Samson leans on them. Philadelphian Christians
might live in fear of earthquake shocks, but nothing will shake
them when they stand as pillars in heaven.

So become a pilgrim in this life, and you will be a pillar in
the next. Dare to go out through the door of service, and you
will never go out of the security of paradise. Risk your name for
Christ in this world, and on your pillar in the next world will
be permanently inscribed three names. The first will be the name
of God, the second of the New Jerusalem (the Church Triumphant), and the third will be Christ's new name, for of them you
will continually learn and to them you will eternally belong.
Have no continuing city now, and the New Jerusalem will
be your abode in glory. Be content to wander as a sheep in and
out finding pasture, and you will dwell in the house of the Lord
for ever. That is the prospect before all those who will go forth
valiantly through open doors, wage war for Christ against the
powers of evil and conquer in the fight. It is the promise of
Christ; it is true.

So we conclude another letter, with its astonishingly relevant
message to our own day. The open door stands for the Church's
opportunity; the key of David for Christ's authority; and the
pillar in God's temple for the conqueror's security. Christ has the
keys. Christ has opened the doors. Christ promises to make us
safe as massive pillars in a temple. Now it is up to us. The
doors stand open to invite us. Let us not hesitate a moment
longer. Let us go in through the door of salvation, and out
through the door of service.

8

THE LETTER
TO LAODICEA: WHOLEHEARTEDNESS
(Rev. 3: 14-22)

AND to the angel of the church in Laodicea write: "The words of the Amen, the faithful and true witness, the beginning of God's creation. I know your works: you are neither cold nor hot. Would that you were cold or hot! So, because you are lukewarm, and neither cold nor hot, I will spew you out of my mouth. For you say, I am rich, I have prospered, and I need nothing; not knowing that you are wretched, pitiable, poor, blind, and naked. Therefore I counsel you to buy from me gold refined by fire, that you may be rich, and white garments to clothe you and to keep the shame of your nakedness from being seen, and salve to anoint your eyes, that you may see. Those whom I love, I reprove and chasten; so be zealous and repent. Behold, I stand at the door and knock; if any one hears my voice and opens the door, I will come in to him and eat with him, and he with me. He who conquers, I will grant him to sit with me on my throne, as I myself conquered and sat down with my Father on his throne. He who has an ear, let him hear what the Spirit says to the churches."

In each of the seven letters Christ lays emphasis on a different mark which should characterize a true and living church. The Ephesian Christians are urged to return to their first, fresh love for Him, while the Christians of Smyrna are warned that if they do not compromise they will surely suffer. The church in Pergamum is to champion truth in the face of error, and the church in Thyatira is to follow righteousness in the midst of evil. In Sardis the need is for inward reality behind the church's outward show. Before the Philadelphian church the risen Lord has set an open door of opportunity for the spread of the gospel, and He bids them step boldly through it. The seventh letter is addressed to the church in Laodicea and combines with a fierce denunciation of complacency a tender appeal for whole-heartedness.

About forty miles south-east of Philadelphia three famous cities clustered in the valley of the River Lycus. North of the river stood Hierapolis, while on its south bank were situated Laodicea and Colosse, about ten miles distant from each other. Laodicea was thus the most southerly of the seven churches to which these letters were addressed, being almost due east of Ephesus.

Although Laodicea was the chief city of the southern region of Phrygia and of no mean distinction, nobody knows when the seeds of the gospel were sown in it or how the Christian Church took root there. St. Paul probably never visited the cities of the Lycus valley, and it is possible that Epaphras founded the church. But Paul wrote a letter to the Laodicean church at the same time as he wrote his epistle to the Colossians. Indeed, most contemporary scholars think that the Laodicean letter is none other than our so-called "Epistle to the Ephesians" since three of the best and earliest manuscripts of that epistle omit at its beginning the words, "at Ephesus". It may therefore have been a circular letter sent in the first instance to Laodicea (Col. 1: 7; 2: 1; 4: 12–16).

Whenever it had been founded, and however it may have prospered in its early history, the church in Laodicea had now fallen on evil days, and Jesus Christ sends to it the sternest of the seven letters, containing much censure and no praise. The church had not been infected with the poison of any special sin or error. We read neither of heretics nor of persecutors. But the Christians in Laodicea were *neither cold nor hot* (v. 15). They lacked wholeheartedness, so that the adjective "Laodicean" has passed into our language to describe somebody who is lukewarm in religion or politics and any other sphere.

The Laodicean church was a halfhearted church. Perhaps none of the seven letters is more appropriate to the twentieth-century church than this. It describes vividly the respectable, sentimental, nominal, skin-deep religiosity which is so widespread among us today. Our Christianity is flabby and anaemic. We appear to have taken a lukewarm bath of religion. In this phrase there is probably, wrote Professor H. B. Swete (p. 59), "an allusion to the hot springs of Hierapolis, which in their way over the plateau become lukewarm, and in this condition discharge themselves over the cliff right opposite to Laodicea".

Laodicean religion is like a lukewarm waterfall. But Jesus Christ deserves better treatment than this. He wants His followers to be either cold or hot. *I know your works*, He says; *you are neither cold nor hot. Would that you were cold or hot!* (v. 15). The Greek words are striking, and we are left in no doubt about their meaning. "Cold" means icy cold and "hot" means boiling hot. Jesus Christ would prefer us to boil or to freeze, rather than that we should simmer down into a tasteless tepidity. Paul told the Roman Christians to be what he had found Apollos to be, namely "fervent in spirit" or spiritually at boiling point. We are to "maintain the spiritual glow", as Moffatt translated this exhortation, and to "rekindle" or "stir into flame" the gift of God that is in us. Our inner spiritual fire is in constant danger of dying down. It needs to be poked and fed and fanned into flame (Rom. 12: 11; Acts 18: 25; 2 Tim. 1: 6).

The idea of being on fire for Christ will strike some people as dangerous emotionalism. "Surely", they will say, "we are not meant to go to extremes? You are not asking us to become hot-gospel fanatics?" Well, wait a minute. It depends what you mean. If by "fanaticism" you really mean "wholeheartedness" then Christianity is a fanatical religion and every Christian should be a fanatic. But fanaticism is not wholeheartedness, nor is wholeheartedness fanaticism. Fanaticism is an unreasoning and unintelligent wholeheartedness. It is the running away of the heart with the head. At the end of a statement prepared for a conference on science, philosophy and religion at Princeton University in 1940 came these words: "Commitment without reflexion is fanaticism in action; but reflexion without commitment is the paralysis of all action." What Jesus Christ desires and deserves is the reflexion which leads to commitment and the commitment which is born of reflexion. This is the meaning of wholeheartedness, of being aflame for God.

One longs today to see robust and virile men and women bringing to Jesus Christ their thoughtful and their total commitment. Jesus Christ asks for this. He even says that if we will not be hot, He would prefer us cold to lukewarm. Better be frigid than tepid, He implies. His meaning is not far to seek. If He is true; if He is the Son of God who died for the sins of men; if Christmas Day, Good Friday and Easter Day are more than meaningless anniversaries, then nothing less than our wholehearted commitment to Christ will do. I must put Him first in my private and public life, seeking His glory and obeying His will. Better be icy in my indifference or go into active opposition to Him than insult Him with an insipid compromise which nauseates Him!

True, the Christian Church has often been scared stiff of "enthusiasm". John Wesley and his friends had reason to know this. So have many others both before him and since. But enthusiasm is an essential part of Christianity. Christ warmly approves of it even if the Church disapproves. His message to us in our sleepyheaded lethargy and chilliness is His message to Laodicea years ago: *be zealous and repent* (v. 19). Zeal, heat, fire, passion—these are the qualities we lack today and desperately need.

We must consider carefully what Christ says about halfheartedness as He explains what it is, how to overcome it and the reward He promises to the wholehearted.

(1) THE DIAGNOSIS CHRIST MAKES

We shall need to brace ourselves and hold tight. We may be in for a shock. *You say, I am rich, I have prospered, and I need nothing; not knowing that you are wretched, pitiable, poor, blind, and naked* (v. 17). Here is the diagnosis of the Good Physician. The tepid person is one in whom there is a glaring contrast between what he says and thinks he is on the one hand and what he really is on the other. The root cause of half heartedness is complacency. To be lukewarm is to be blind to one's true condition.

No doubt the congregation of Laodicea teemed with self-satisfied churchgoers. They said *I am rich, I have prospered, and I need nothing*. They were quite right—in material things. Laodicea was renowned for its prosperity. Situated in a fertile valley and at the junction of several important trade routes, it had amassed considerable wealth. So opulent were its citizens that, when the earthquake of A.D. 60 devastated the whole region, the city was promptly rebuilt without any appeal to the Roman senate for the customary subsidy. The local inhabitants were proud of their city as a mercantile banking centre. They could boast of its famous medical school connected with the temple of Aesculapius "whose physicians prepared the Phrygian powder for the cure of ophthalmia" (*Westminster Dictionary of the Bible*), which was described by Aristotle. Particularly illustrious was their manufacture of cloth, garments and carpets from the valuable wool of the local sheep, which Professor Ramsay says was "soft in texture and glossy black in colour" (*The Letters to the Seven Churches of Asia*, p. 416).

The pride of Laodicea was infectious. Christians caught the plague. The spirit of complacency crept into the church and tainted it. Members of the church became smug and self-satisfied, and Jesus Christ needed bluntly to expose them. He did not mince His words. *You say, I am rich, I have prospered, and I need nothing; not knowing that you are wretched, pitiable, poor, blind, and naked* (v. 17). They thought they were doing fine in their religious life. But Christ had to describe them as blind and naked beggars—beggars despite their banks, blind despite the Phrygian powders of their medical school, and naked despite their clothing factories. *I need nothing*, they said. They could indeed manage without an imperial subsidy; but they could not manage without the grace of Jesus Christ.

This then is Christ's view of us—of the nominal Christian who is neither really nor wholeheartedly committed to Him. Morally and spiritually such a person is a naked, blind beggar. He is a beggar because he has nothing with which to purchase his forgiveness or an entry into the Kingdom of God. He is naked because he has no clothes to fit him to stand before God. He is blind because he has no idea either of his spiritual poverty or of his spiritual danger.

Such is the ascended Christ's penetrating diagnosis of our spiritual condition. Do we resist it? To contradict the diagnosis of a skilled physician is the surest road to disaster. "I know thy works" He says, and adds "thou . . . knowest not" (verses 15 and 17 A.V.). We tend to flatter and deceive ourselves, but He sees and knows us as we really are.

(2) THE ADVICE CHRIST GIVES

Therefore I counsel you . . . (v. 18). Perhaps we could first observe the fact that we have a God who is content to give advice to His creatures. I can never read this verse without being strangely moved. He is the great God of the immense, unfathomable universe. He has countless galaxies of stars at His fingertips. The heaven and the heaven of heavens cannot contain Him. He is the creator and sustainer of all things, the Lord God Almighty. He has the right to issue orders for us to obey; He prefers to give advice which we need not heed. He could command; He chooses to counsel. He respects the freedom with which He has ennobled us.

At the same time He warns us of the serious consequences of

our complacency. His purpose is not to terrify us into submission, but to enforce upon us the solemnity of our choice. *Because you are lukewarm, and neither cold nor hot, I will spew you out of my mouth* (v. 16). It is of course metaphorical language, but this does not empty the expression of its meaning. Lukewarm liquids create nausea. They are not only tasteless but positively distasteful. Christ's forceful expression is one of disgust. He will utterly repudiate those whose attachment to Him is purely nominal and superficial. One is reminded of the description in Psalm 95 of God's attitude to Israel in the wilderness: "Forty years long was I grieved with this generation" (v. 10 A.V.). The verb used is almost shocking. The Revised Standard Version translates it "loathed". Of course God's wrath is never tinged with personal malice or spiteful vindictiveness. But I understand that the Hebrew word employed in this psalm conveys distaste and disgust, and indicates God's strong moral indignation at man's hypocrisy and sin.

Whether or not the Laodicean church heeded this warning we cannot say. Certainly the city, once prosperous and complacent, is now a miserable waste. "Nothing can exceed the desolation and melancholy appearance of the site of Laodicea", says a recent traveller (C. J. Vaughan, *Lectures on the Revelation*, pp. 101-2). Archbishop Trench vividly portrays the scene: "All has perished now. He who removed the candlestick of Ephesus, has rejected Laodicea out of His mouth. The fragments of aqueducts and theatres spread over a vast extent of country tell of the former magnificence of this city; but of this once famous church nothing survives" (pp. 190-191).

It is not only, however, through fear of judgment that we should heed this divine warning, but also from respect for the One who issues it. See how He describes Himself in the introduction to this epistle: *The words of the Amen, the faithful and true witness, the beginning of God's creation* (v. 14). He is *the Amen*. This Hebrew word is an adverb of assent. It means "indeed" or "verily", and denotes the confirmation of something said or done. This is the word employed by Jesus in His favourite formula "Verily, verily I say unto you". But now He not only says "Amen"; He *is* the Amen. His ministry fulfils all the promises of God, "'for all the promises of God find their Yes in Him" (2 Cor. 1: 20). His words are reliable because of His steadfast character. He is neither fickle nor capricious. No idle whim ever moves Him to speak or act. He has never needed to retract ·or modify any statement which He has made. He is absolutely consistent. Moreover, He is *the faithful and true witness* (v. 14, cf. 1: 5). His words are true and therefore trustworthy. "We speak of what we know" He claimed in His conversation with Nicodemus "and bear witness to what we have seen" (Jn. 3: 11). Therefore His witness should be received. It is accurate and dependable. Again, He is *the beginning of God's creation*. If we adopt the fundamental principle of Biblical interpretation that each Scripture must be understood in the light of all and that no passage may be so expounded "that it be repugnant to another" (Church of England Article XX, "Of the Authority of the Church"), then this title of Christ means "the originator of the creation of God". It is reminiscent of phrases in the Epistle to the Colossians (1: 15, 18) with which the Laodicean Christians were no doubt familiar. The Bible teaches that Jesus the Eternal Word was the agent of the Father's creative activity, and that though all things are "from" the Father, they are "through" the Son. Christ is thus Himself "the uncreated principle of creation". Yet it is of the creation *of God* that He is the beginning—an expression which "reserves the supreme proprietorship for the Father" (Swete pp. 58 and 59).

Such is Christ, *the Amen*, *the faithful and true witness*, *the beginning of God's creation*. How can we ignore the advice of such a Being? He cannot lie. He knows and tells the truth. It would be the height of lunacy to disregard His counsel.

What then is His advice? *I counsel you to buy from me. . . .* We pause again a moment. We must not miss the emphasis which is laid on the words *from me*. It was this above all that the Laodiceans had to learn. They considered themselves selfsufficient; they must humbly find their sufficiency in Christ. They were saying *I need nothing*; they must come to admit that their need was great and that only Christ could supply it. They said "*I* am rich, *I* have prospered, and *I* need nothing". Jesus Christ had to humble that boastful personal pronoun and lay it in the dust, and say "it is *from Me* that your salvation comes". He might have echoed God's words to Ephraim "from me comes your fruit" or His own statement to the twelve "apart from me you can do nothing" (Hos. 14: 8; Jn. 15: 5).

But why does He recommend the Laodiceans to *buy* from Him? Can salvation be bought? No. Certainly not. It is a free gift to us because it was purchased by Christ on the cross. His invitation "buy from me" should not be pressed. He is doubtless using language appropriate to the commercially-minded Laodiceans. He likens Himself to a merchant who visits the city to sell his wares and goes into competition with other salesmen. "I advise you to forsake your former suppliers", says the Divine Colporteur, "and come trade with me". Perhaps also He is thinking of Jehovah's appeal: "Ho, every one who thirsts, come to the waters; and he who has no money, come, buy and eat! Come, buy wine and milk without money and without price" (Is. 55: 1).

So Christ continues. *I counsel you to buy from me gold refined by fire, that you may be rich, and white garments to clothe you and to keep the shame of your nakedness from being seen, and salve to anoint your eyes, that you may see* (v. 18). Here is welcome news for naked, blind beggars! They are poor; but Christ has gold. They are naked; but Christ has clothes. They are blind; but Christ has eyesalve. Let them no longer trust in their banks, their Phrygian eyepowders and their clothing factories! Let them come to Him! He can enrich their poverty, clothe their nakedness and heal their blindness. He can open their eyes to perceive a spiritual world of which they have never even dreamed. He can cover their sin and shame and make them fit to partake of the inheritance of the saints in light. He can enrich them with life and life abundant. In a word, He can save them. He has died for them and risen again. Through His death they can be cleansed and through His living presence within them they can be changed.

But how could this come about? The Laodiceans must take two steps. The first is given in verse 19. The Lord Jesus goes on: *Those whom I love, I reprove and chasten; so be zealous and repent.* The first step is repentance. Already Christ has called on those in Ephesus and Sardis to repent (2: 5; 3: 3). The same message is addressed to Laodicea. There can be no glossing over this charge. The Christ who warns them that He will spit them out of His mouth if they do not stir themselves, yet loves them. Indeed it is because He longs to save them from final judgment that He now reproves and chastens them. They must *be zealous and repent.* The tenses change significantly. Let them repent at once and irrevocably; then let them continue always to be fired with zeal. To repent is to turn with resolution from all that is known to be contrary to God's will. Like the Laodiceans we must renounce the old life of easygoing complacency. Smug self-satisfaction does not become one who claims the name of Christ. Shallow piety never saved any man. There will be no hypocrites in heaven. Then let us break with these things. Let us spit them out of our mouths lest He spit us out of His.

So the first step is repentance. The second step is faith. Exactly what the commitment is which the New Testament calls faith is now clearly and vividly described by Jesus Christ. *Behold, I stand at the door and knock; if any one hears my voice and opens the door, I will come in to him and eat with him, and he with me* (v. 20). You will have noticed that this is a personal appeal. These words are addressed not to the church but to the individual. *If any one . . .,* Christ says. Our heart or soul is likened to a dwelling. You have yours, and I have mine. Each of us likes to rule his own roost and be king of his own castle. But the living Christ comes to visit us. He who threatens that He may have to spit us from His mouth now stands on our front doorstep. He knocks. He wants to be admitted. It is a visit from the Lover of our soul. The love scene in the Song of Solomon repeats itself. "Hark! my Beloved is knocking: 'Open to me, my sister, my love, my dove, my perfect one. . . .' My Beloved put his hand to the latch, and my heart was thrilled within me. I arose to open to my Beloved. . . ." (5:2-5).

If we do open the door of our heart to Jesus Christ and let Him in, He will bring an end to our beggary. He will transform us from paupers into princes. He will cleanse us and clothe us. He will sup with us, and we shall be permitted to sup with Him. The picture illustrates the shared joys of the Christian life, the reciprocal fellowship which the Christian has with his Saviour. That He should bid us come and sup with Him is honour enough; but that He should wish to share our humble board and sup with us is wonder beyond our finite understanding. We are not worthy that He should come under our roof, and will He sit at our table? Of this inward festive meal the Lord's Supper is the outward and visible sacrament. To eat bread and drink wine is but a physical representation of the spiritual feast with Christ and on Christ which His people are privileged continuously to enjoy. To kneel at His table in a church sets forth publicly our private supping with Him in our hearts. And both the inward feast and the sacramental supper are a foretaste of that heavenly banquet which in the Book of the Revelation is called "the marriage supper of the Lamb" (Rev. 19: 9; cf. Lk. 22: 30).

But it is not merely for supper that Christ enters the human soul. It is also to exercise sovereignty. If He comes in to bestow His salvation, He comes in also to receive our submission. His entry is an occupation. He comes in to take control. No room may be locked against Him. He has conquered us. His flag flies from our roof. He is the master of the house. This is what it means to be committed to Christ, and to be wholehearted in our allegiance to Him. It is to surrender without terms to His lordship. It is to seek His will in His word and promptly to obey it.

It is not just attending religious services, twice a Sunday or even every day, let alone on the major festivals. It is not just leading a decent life or believing certain articles of the creed. No, no. It is first to repent, turning decisively from everything we know to be wrong, and then to open the door to Jesus Christ, asking Him to come in. It is getting our gold and our clothes and our eyesalve from Him. It is being personally and unconditionally committed to Him. It is putting Him first and seeking His pleasure in every department of life, public and private. Nothing less will do.

Are you hot, cold or tepid? It depends on whether you have opened the door of your whole personality to the Lord Jesus Christ. Have you ever done this? If not, will you do it today? It is only the beginning of the Christian life; but it is an indispensable beginning.

(3) THE PROSPECT CHRIST OFFERS

Like the previous six letters, the letter to the Laodicean church concludes with a gracious promise to the conqueror, to the man or woman, that is, who hears and heeds and obeys Christ's message. *He who conquers, I will grant him to sit with me on my throne, as I myself conquered and sat down with my Father on His throne* (v. 21). This prospect exceeds in glory all the other promises to the conqueror. A throne is the symbol of conquest and authority. Jesus had promised the twelve that "in the new world", when the Son of man would "sit on His glorious throne" they who had followed Him would "also sit on twelve thrones, judging the twelve tribes of Israel" (Mt. 19: 28). This pledge is now given to every faithful and conquering Christian. As Christ conquered the world and the devil, and was exalted to the Father's right hand, so the Christian conqueror shall be honoured also. As Christ shares the Father's throne, so the Christian will share Christ's. Exactly what authority will be entrusted to him is not disclosed, but in some way he will be given responsibility in the Kingdom of heaven.

If we let Christ enter the house of our heart, He will let us enter the house of His Father. Further, if we allow Christ to sit with us at our table, He will allow us to sit with Him on His throne.

Here then is the great alternative which confronts every thoughtful person. To be halfhearted, complacent and only casually interested in the things of God is to prove oneself not a Christian at all and to be so distasteful to Christ as to be in danger of a vehement rejection. But to be wholehearted in one's devotion to Christ, having opened the door and submitted without reserve to Him, is to be given the privilege both of supping with Him on earth and of reigning with Him in heaven. Here is a choice we cannot avoid. We must either throw the door open to Him or keep it closed in His face.

The last verse of the chapter reads: *He who has an ear, let him hear what the Spirit says to the churches* (v. 22). These words are repeated without alteration as a postscript to each letter. They are reminiscent of a characteristic expression which Jesus used during His ministry: "He who has ears to hear, let him hear" (e.g. Mk. 4: 9). The phrase in the Revelation is almost identical, and only adds *what the Spirit says to the churches*. The letters are dictated by Christ, but the message is the word of the Spirit. He who spoke through the prophets in olden days and through apostles in the New Testament revelation is now the agent of the Son's charge to the churches.

It is noteworthy also that although each letter is addressed to a different church, the concluding formula refers to *the churches*. The personal message to each is yet a general challenge to all. The message varies according to the circumstances of each congregation but not according to the purpose of the Divine Writer. His will for His Church is the same, for every congregation of every age and every place. We have seen what Christ thinks of the Church, and what His ideal for it is. It would be sinful folly to turn a deaf ear to this urgent message. *He who has an ear, let him hear what the Spirit says to the churches.*

9

CONCLUSION

WE have seen what Christ thinks of His Church. We have considered the marks which should characterize it— love for Christ and willingness to suffer for Him, truth of doctrine and holiness of life, inward reality and an evangelistic outreach to others, with an uncompromising wholeheartedness in everything. We have watched it hard pressed by sin, error and lethargy within, and by tribulation and persecution without. We have heard of the evil designs and deeds of the Nicolaitans, the Balaamites and the woman Jezebel. We have caught many glimpses of the dilemma between Christ and Caesar which had been forced upon Asian Christians. It was hard for them to stand firm in the midst of opposition.

But we cannot leave them thus. With chapter four of the Book of Revelation we turn from the Church on earth to the Church in heaven, from Christ among the flickering lampstands to Christ near the unchangeable throne of God. *After this I looked*, John writes, *and lo, in heaven an open door!* (4: 1). Through this door of revelation he looked, and his eye lighted on the symbol of the sovereignty of God. *And lo, a throne stood in heaven, with One seated on the throne!* (4: 2).

The churches of Asia were small and struggling; the might of Rome was inexhaustible. What could a few defenceless Christians do if an imperial edict were to banish them from the face of the earth? Already the powers of darkness seemed to be closing in upon them. The hearts of Christians began to tremble like the trees of the forest in the wind.

Yet they need have no fear. At the centre of the universe is a throne. From it the wheeling planets receive their orders. To it gigantic galaxies give their allegiance. In it the tiniest living organism finds its life. Before it angels and men and all created things in heaven above and earth beneath bow down and humbly worship. The Lord God omnipotent reigns!

The next chapters of the Book of Revelation (4 to 7) leave us in no doubt about the security of the people of God. The Eternal Father sits on His throne, surrounded by the worshipping host of heaven. The Book of Destiny is in the hand of Christ, and no calamity can befall mankind unless He breaks the seals of the book. The winds of judgment will not blow upon those who have been sealed by the Holy Spirit. These are the symbols of divine sovereignty. The Church's security is guaranteed by the Holy Trinity.

So ultimately, when we have fought a good fight and finished our course, and even if need be suffered death for the name of Christ, we shall emerge from the great tribulation and suffer no more. The King of the universe will grant us refuge in the shelter of His throne, where we may see Him and worship Him day and night in His temple, and the Lamb turned Shepherd will lead us with the rest of His sheep to fountains of living water, where we may slake our thirst for ever at the eternal springs.